THE MIND *of* YOUR STORY

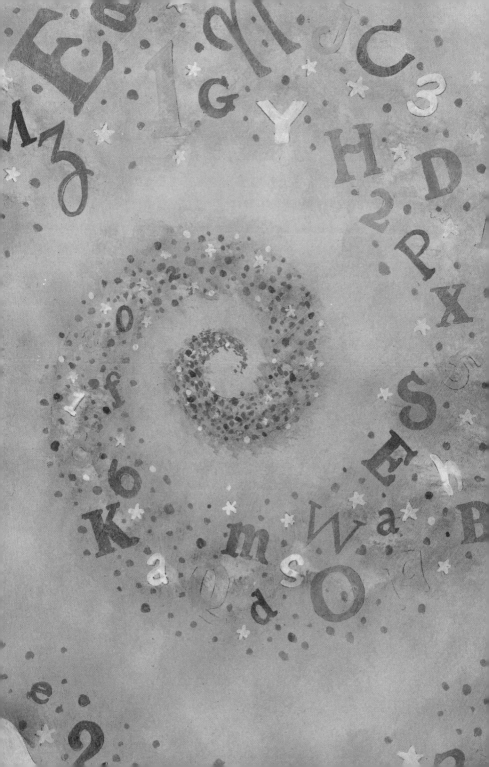

THE MIND *of* YOUR STORY

discover what drives your fiction

LISA LENARD-COOK

WRITER'S DIGEST BOOKS
Cincinnati, Ohio
www.writersdigest.com

For more fine books from F+W Publications, visit www.fwpublications.com.

12 11 10 09 08   5 4 3 2 1

Distributed in Canada by Fraser Direct, 100 Armstrong Avenue, Georgetown, ON, Canada L7G 5S4, Tel: (905) 877-4411. Distributed in the U.K. and Europe by David & Charles, Brunel House, Newton Abbot, Devon, TQ12 4PU, England, Tel: (+44) 1626 323200, Fax: (+44) 1626 323319, E-mail: postmaster@davidandcharles.co.uk. Distributed in Australia by Capricorn Link, P.O. Box 704, Windsor, NSW 2756 Australia, Tel: (02) 4577-3555.

Visit Writersdigest.com for information on more resources for writers. To receive a free weekly e-mail newsletter delivering tips and updates about writing and about Writer's Digest products, register directly at http://newsletters.fwpublications.com.

Some of the material included in this book originally appeared, in various forms, in "The Art of Fiction," the author's monthly column at Authorlink.com, and in *Sage*, the monthly newsletter of SouthWest Writers.

Library of Congress Cataloging-in-Publication Data

Lenard-Cook, Lisa.
  The mind of your story : discover what drives your fiction / by Lisa Lenard-Cook. --1st ed.
    p. cm.
  Includes bibliographical references and index.
  ISBN 978-1-58297-488-0 (hardcover : alk. paper)
    1. Fiction--Authorship. 2. Plots (Drama, novel, etc.) 3. Narration (Rhetoric) I. Title.
  PN3378.L35 2008
  808.3--dc22   2007040435

Edited by Lauren Mosko
Designed by Grace Ring
Production coordinated by Mark Griffin
Illustrations on selected pages © Photodisc / Getty Images

Acknowledgments

A huge thank you to the folks at Writer's Digest Books, in particular my partner in revision, Lauren Mosko. Thanks, too, to Anne Hawkins, Doris Booth, Beth Hadas, Judy Villella, Kaitlin Kushner, and my husband Bob Cook, as well as Mr. Bones and Stellaluna, office guardians. Most of all, thanks to my students, who keep on asking the questions that get me started all over again.

About the Author

Lisa Lenard-Cook's first novel, *Dissonance* (University of New Mexico Press), won the Jim Sagel Award for the Novel while still in manuscript and went on to be short-listed for the PEN Southwest Book Award. The book was also a selection of the Durango-La Plata County Reads! countywide reading program and NPR Performance Today's Summer Reading Series. Her second novel, *Coyote Morning* (UNM Press), was short-listed for the New Mexico Press Women's Zia Award and, like *Dissonance*, a Southwest Book of the Year. Lisa is on the faculty of the Santa Barbara Writers Conference and is the fiction columnist for the Web site Authorlink.com. Visit her Web site, www.lisalenardcook.com, for information on upcoming appearances and classes. Lisa lives in Corrales, New Mexico.

TABLE *of* CONTENTS

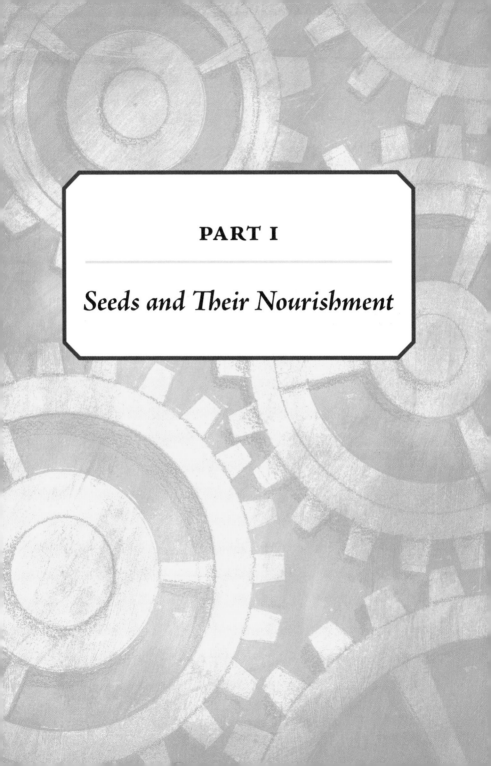

PART I

Seeds and Their Nourishment

chapter 1
FICTIONAL SEEDS

It's a dark and stormy night. No, really. It *is*. You're driving home from, say, a PTA meeting, and the rain is turning to snow. As you turn a familiar corner, your headlights illuminate a woman struggling along the side of the road, dragging a suitcase.

You can't help it. You pull over. You ask her if she wants a ride. She shakes her head. You insist. She shakes her head more vehemently. Then she's gone.

You pull back onto the road. *Where was she going?* you wonder. Where was she coming from? And why was she out on such a night in the first place? Why did she refuse your offer of a ride? As you drive home (slowly, now; the streets are growing slick with sleet), you can almost see the fight with an abusive husband that must have been the last straw. Or perhaps it was a parent—it's possible she was still a teen. After all, you didn't get a good look at her ....

But why a fight? Perhaps her car broke down and she won't accept rides from strangers, even benign parents on their way home from PTA meetings. But what if she's not so benign herself? It's possible she just killed that abusive husband and the last thing she wants is for someone else to note her existence, someone who might pin her to the neighborhood of the crime. She couldn't help it, of course. It was an accident ....

Except now, *you've* seen her, and so the police could come looking for you, the one person who saw her on this dark and stormy night ....

And so, it begins: the obsessive round-and-round that is the mind of a fiction writer. If you've ever wondered where we get our ideas, you're probably not a fiction writer yourself. Those of us who are were born obsessing, worrying over things that most people (people we writers know are far more "normal" than we) don't even register. My husband's one of those normal people, and having him around is wonderfully grounding. But that doesn't mean images like that woman don't get stuck in my head. In fact, while I've changed some details, I did once stop for a woman with a suitcase on a blizzardy night in southwest Colorado, a woman who turned down my offer of a ride.

Things That Get Stuck in Our Heads

I use the word "stuck" intentionally because when I visualize what happens when I obsess, I not only see a needle stuck in a groove on a 33⅓ record, I hear the repetitive oddity such a scratch creates. (Those younger than I am have heard this sound re-created more recently by DJs but may not realize its origin in mechanical malfunction.) For those of us who grew up listening to records, carefully picking up the needle and setting it down just past the offending scratch was something we did so often it never occurred to us it took some skill and finesse.

That repetition, that over-and-over with no way out unless someone physically lifts the needle from the groove, is how it is when something gets stuck in a writer's head. She'll start thinking about something she said (or wishes she said), or did, or saw, like that woman with the suitcase in the rain. She starts spinning the thing out, imagining what comes next. But then she gets to a certain point—and it's always the same point—and she skips right back to the beginning.

These ruts can be maddening, and in fact, if we weren't writers, they likely *would* drive us insane. But when we write, there are things we can *do* with them. Writing teachers like Natalie Goldberg and Julia Cameron suggest writing such obsessions down just as they are, as soon as you realize they're spinning out of control. Cameron proposes what she calls "morning pages": three unfiltered pages written first thing in the morning as soon as you get up, before coffee, before conversation, before any daytime thoughts enter in to filter (that is, edit) your nighttime rambles. Goldberg similarly urges writers to just write, to, as she puts it in *Writing Down the Bones*, "Keep your hand moving …" without "thinking" or "logic." Pay attention to those words, *thinking* and *logic*. I'll return to them in a moment.

Because of the way my own mind operates, I don't write such things down—not right away, anyway. Instead, when I realize something's stuck, that I'm going to wear it out with the going over, I "send it over to right brain" to become what I call a fictional seed.

Right Brain/Left Brain (Or, Left Brain/Right Brain)

There are many books that discuss the hemispheres of the brain, so I'm not going to spend a lot of time on the details. I refer you in particular to Betty Edwards's *Drawing on the Right Side of the Brain*, which has as much to tell writers as it does artists, and which itself relies on the primary research of Roger W. Sperry, who in 1981 was awarded the Nobel Prize for his pioneering work in hemispheric brain study. For the purposes of our discussion, though, I want to talk about what happens to obsessions in the right brain and how we can learn to translate these seeds into fiction.

The right hemisphere of the brain is visual and holistic, the place of dreams and schemes, creativity and desire. You can think of it as your inner child, if you like that sort of imagery, or simply the place where you get to, as Julia Cameron phrases it, "make a mess." The brain's left hemisphere is more logical and analytical; it sees—insists on—the order of things and is good at getting things done. It's also where language resides. For most of us raised in western countries, left brain represents our conscious and right brain our unconscious. In my own effort to simplify this concept, I call what left brain does "thinking" and what happens in right brain "knowing." That's because thinking is an orderly process we can retrace if need be, while knowing simply *is*.

What this dichotomy suggests is that writers have to open the channel between right brain, where ideas germinate, and left brain, where they get translated into words. I believe that much writing breaks down in this translation because we haven't been taught how to allow the hemispheres of our brain to "talk" to each other. Think of an engineer (left brain) and an artist (right brain) trying to communicate, and you begin to see the quandary.

Over the years, I've learned that when something gets stuck in my head (if it's stuck, it's left brain where it happens), I can "send it over to right brain," where ideas can flower without my conscious knowledge. I've also learned that three seemingly unrelated seeds must somehow rub against each other in right brain before a fiction will begin.

It's possible (in fact, it's likely) that your brain doesn't work precisely the way mine does. For one thing, I have an eidetic memory (this is a fancy term for a photographic memory), which means I can pull up "images" of things I've seen and "recordings" of things I've heard. Eidetic memory, research shows, is genetic (like me, my mother once believed that everyone has this capability and, also like me, was startled to learn that most do not), and it's a marvelous tool for a writer. It provides us with an attic full of resources from which we can cull what we need, when we need it.

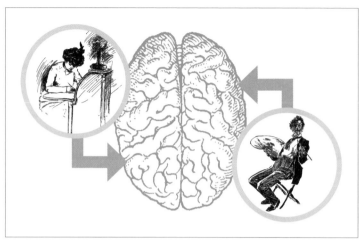

Left brain "thinks." Right brain "knows."

If you haven't got an eidetic memory, though, you'll likely need to post reminders to yourself, and these reminders may well take the form of the jottings that Goldberg and Cameron encourage. Simply writing your obsessions down is often enough to yank them from their repetitive (left brain) ruts, just as, for me, sending them over to right brain does the trick. It will amount to the same thing: The obsessions won't go away; they'll simply relocate so the mysterious work of the unconscious can begin.

There are a number of ways to go about recording and filing these jottings. You can write each down on a slip of paper and then drop each slip into a place you've reserved for them. This can be anything from a file folder to a three-ring notebook to a fishbowl to a pretty box. (Writers love boxes. They're visual reminders of our subliminal selves.) Or, you can use one of those gorgeous notebooks you've been saving until you had something fabulous to write in it. (You know the one.)

It's possible three seeds sent to right brain in one of these ways will rub against each other and spark in the same way I've described above. But you can also try rubbing them against each other yourself by reaching into your fishbowl or file (or flipping through your gorgeous notebook) and seeing what happens when you start a fiction with three seemingly unrelated seeds.

Right Brain Magic

What happens in right brain is something methodical left brain (who translates all this into words and language) can't easily explain, but I'll try nonetheless. In *Drawing on the Right Side of the Brain*, Betty Edwards calls the process "magical," and the way things suddenly fall into place when sent from right brain to left does, in fact, seem "pulled from thin air." But two very different examples serve to illustrate what's really happening in right brain.

The first is that lost set of keys. You know the ones. You swear you put them on the counter, but they're nowhere to be found. And you're late, of course, and you haven't got a clue where your spare set is, either. Furious, frustrated, you look in every possible nook and cranny, pocket and purse, even in the powder room and the pantry. Finally, you give up. You're not going to find them. You call your appointment and apologize, explain why you can't make it. You take off your coat, maybe change into sweats. You pour a glass of wine and settle down with that book you've been meaning to read. And suddenly, right there on the page of the book, it seems, you can see the keys in the pocket of the navy blazer you wore last night. Sure enough, when you get up to check, there they are.

So why couldn't you think of this when you were frantically trying to find those keys? The answer, not surprisingly, can be found in the language itself: Because you were *thinking*. Thinking, remember, is a left-brain activity, and when it's particularly all-consuming, which it is when you're frantic, right brain can't get a word—or, in right brain's case, an image—in edge-wise. But as soon as you engage left brain in a less stressful activity—settling down with that book, for example—right brain takes the opportunity to—*nyah-nyah!*—let you know *it* knew the answer all along.

Betty Edwards describes it this way: "In order to gain access to [the right brain], it is necessary to present the brain with a job that the verbal, analytic [left brain] will turn down." So, too, with jobs left brain can't handle, instead going into endless loop. Turning these obsessions into fictional seeds is a job that "visual, perceptual" right brain relishes.

This is why it seems as if your best ideas always come when you're in the shower, driving, gardening, jogging, or similarly involved in some physical activity. What happens is that when you engage left brain in an endeavor that requires its focus, right brain can send its images over without left brain trying to interpret (or censor) them in its own distinct way.

This leads us to my second example, dreams. How many times have you awoken from one and said, "Now that was a weird dream." Whenever someone begins telling a dream this way, I gently remind him that dreams aren't "weird"; they just seem that way to logical left brain when it tries to interpret them, because the imagery of dreams is the language of right brain, not easily translated into the dominant language of left brain.

Unless, that is, you're a writer. This brings us to the crux of what I'm trying to say. If you've ever had the experience of a character or story "taking over" during your writing time, you already know what it feels like when right brain is given free rein: Time (a left-brain concept), you (a left-brain concept), and the world around you (a left-brain concept) all cease to exist. Right brain knows exactly what it wants to say and how it wants to say it. And without left brain standing there tapping its metaphorical foot and telling right brain it has no business messing up a good thing, right brain will have a grand time writing the story you really want to tell anyway.

Stirring the Pot

When I send an obsession over to right brain, what I'm really doing is tossing it into a pot. There are a lot of other seeds in that pot already, and I'll get more than one stew (or story) from the resulting broth. What I've learned, though, is that good fiction requires more than one seed.

So how do these seeds become a fiction stew? Here's where my favorite definition of fiction, from Robie Macauley and George Lanning's *Technique in Fiction*, comes into play:

> *"Fiction originates in **direct personal impression** linked by **imagination** with the **writer's resources of experience**." (emphasis mine)*

Let's begin with the first part of this equation, *direct personal impression*, by returning to the woman with the suitcase on that dark and stormy night. What do you remember about her? No, don't go back and check—it doesn't matter if what you remember is something I said or not. "What really happened" is not important to the beginnings (or the middles or ends) of a fiction. What's important is what gets stuck in your head.

As I've said, I call the things that get stuck in my head fictional seeds. Each of these seeds forms one axis of that "direct personal impression" to which Macauley and Lanning refer in the definition above. The thing is, I can't begin to write. Not yet, not with only one seed, because remember, for me, it takes at least three seemingly unrelated seeds before I can begin.

I never know what three seeds will come together to grow a story. I only know that when the moment happens, when the third seed is planted, I am *compelled* to write. After I've illustrated the other two axes of Macauley and Lanning's definition, I'll come back and show you how three such seeds worked for a story of my own.

The second part of the definition is *linked by imagination*. Chances are, when I painted that fictitious woman, you began to imagine a history for her, even if you aren't a fiction writer. We can't help it. Humans are, above all, creatures of imagination, and when we see something we can't explain, we *imagine* an explanation.

You might imagine, for example, that the woman is not who she seems. Why, for one thing, won't she get in the car? It's raining—no, it's turning to snow, for goodness sake! But why is she out on a night like this in the first place? And what's in that suitcase? She can barely lift it off the ground. Oh my! It could be ... Well, you can see my direction. It's only one possible scenario among many, of course.

The last part of Macauley and Lanning's definition is *the writer's resources of experience*. If you've ever laughed or cried, been angry or overjoyed, loved, hated, or anything in between, you have your own resources of experience. And in the best fiction, you use these resources to *translate this emotion* onto the page for the particular fiction you're writing.

That's it. Sounds easy, right? And really, once you realize how it works, it is. Here, I'll draw it for you so right brain can "see" it, too.

fiction =

direct personal impression + imagination + writer's resources of experience

(what you saw)   (obsession)   (your emotions)

Three Seeds = A Story

Now, here's that example I promised you. About fifteen years ago, both a friend's mother and a neighbor in the remote corner of southwest Colorado where I then lived were diagnosed with Alzheimer's disease. I noticed a number of parallels in the two women's behavior: how polite they were; how both seemed to find joy in simple things they could no longer name. As I drove back and forth to Durango every day, I often found my thoughts turning to something one or the other had said or done, trying to imagine what was going through their heads. I spent so much time thinking about them, in fact, I soon realized this obsession was a fictional seed. But I wasn't ready to write—not yet. It was only one seed, so I sent it over to right brain.

Meanwhile, in that drought summer, the fires burned. In the evening, my then-teenage daughter and I would sit on our porch and watch the planes shuttle back and forth to Grand Junction. When a plane dropped its slurry onto the burn, the sky would momentarily flare pink. My daughter, an artist, and I, a writer, would sit entranced, night after night after night. This direct personal impression also became a fictional seed. But it still wasn't enough.

Then, late that summer, I read a story in the *Rocky Mountain News* about wild horses that were starving on government-owned land in New Mexico. According to the article, the Bureau of Land Management believed their only choice was to kill the horses before they became a nuisance to nearby ranchers. This brief news item became the third seed. I know this because as soon as I read it I sat down and wrote the first line of my short story "Wild Horses." This story is included in appendix A.

"Wild Horses" is told from the point of view of a rancher in southwest Colorado whose wife has Alzheimer's. He oscillates between his memories of the woman he married and the daily reality of the woman she's become. In the evenings, they sit on their porch and watch planes ferry slurry to nearby fires. Then, a Bureau of Land Management functionary announces that the wild horses that live in the canyon beyond their ranch are going to be shot. Throughout this story, we see the wife only through the husband's eyes, and yet, because the husband has the use of my imagination and my direct resources of experience about things like bewilderment, anger, and most of all, love, in this story's few pages we are able to connect deeply with these characters and their particular predicament.

Let's review how the three axes work for this story:

+ *Direct personal impressions* (the seeds): Alzheimer's, the fires, the wild horses
+ *Imagination*: this couple—who they were and who they are now
+ *Writer's resources of experience*: bewilderment, anger, love

Fictional seeds can take years to germinate, but ultimately, it really *is* this simple. The key is to trust your instincts enough to allow the magic to happen.

MINDING YOUR STORY
Obsession

What obsesses you? What do you think about during those nights you can't sleep? Are there recurrent "themes" in your life? As you go about your daily life, consider the things that "get stuck in your head." Try writing one (or more) down, or send one over to right brain and see what happens.

chapter 2
I'VE GOT VOICES IN MY HEAD!

Characters. What's a work of fiction without them?

We've all heard writers say (or have said ourselves) that a character "took over a story" or that a story "just wrote itself." This happens because behind such willful imagined beings are fully conceived characters, with individual voices so compelling that they possess not only their author but their readers as well.

Perhaps I'm lucky: I've got voices in my head, and when one of these voices begins speaking, it's all my 120-words-per-minute can do to keep up. Plus, my characters arrive with names, biographies, even astrological signs. If you prefer not to be a veritable Sybil of fiction, however, you'll want to create biographies for your characters before you begin.

Creating Character Biographies

When it comes to characters, the most important question is how to create fictional people who are not only alive on the page but are *more* compelling than the people your readers encounter in their everyday lives.

Part of the answer can be found above: Every character in every work of fiction should have a complete biography. Much of this biography won't make it into your finished work, but you must know everything about your characters. Here we turn to authors Anne Bernays and Pamela Painter and their book of exercises for writers, *What If?* Bernays and

Painter's exercise "What Do You Know About Your Character?" posits all sorts of questions for you to answer. There are the obvious:

+ What's your character's name?
+ How old is your character?
+ Where does your character live?

And there are the less obvious (but a whole lot more fun—and ultimately more revealing):

+ What's your character's sexual history?
+ What's your character's taste in books and music?
+ What kind of car does your character drive?

Get the idea? Of course, there's that all-important astrological sign. After all, another character might ask what it is.

EXERCISING YOUR CHARACTER RIGHTS

Over the years, I've adapted Bernays and Painter's exercise for my own classes. Before I send students off to create their own character, though, we create a character together in class.

This group character exercise isn't quite a free-for-all, although those who shout first (or loudest) get their answers on the whiteboard. Rather, it's an opportunity for students to bond: There's something about arguing about an imagined person's age, occupation, or obsessions that allows people to find out more about each other, as well.

The best thing about this in-class exercise, though, is that by the time a group (or you, on your own) gets past the basics, not only a specific character but also a *story* begins to emerge. After all, it's conflict that drives story, and the conflicts inherent in people, whether real or imagined, become apparent—and more compelling—the more we know about them.

Because you can go to *What If?* for the exercise, I'm not going to reiterate it here. Instead, I offer some additional categories that aren't included in Bernays and Painter's version. Feel free to add categories of your own and subtract any that don't work for you.

CREATING CHARACTERS WHO LIVE AND BREATHE ON THE PAGE

1. In what specific ways is your character different?
2. What's your character's style? How does she dress? Wear her hair? Makeup? Etc.
3. What does your character like and dislike in other people?
4. Describe a room in your character's home.
5. What is your character passionate about?
6. What electronic devices does your character use (cell phone, PC or Mac, iPod)?
7. What was your character's first sexual encounter like?
8. What was your character's most recent sexual encounter like?
9. What are your character's secret ambitions?
10. If your character could have only one thing, be it concrete (a sports car, spouse, or servant) or abstract (fame, beauty, power), what would it be?
11. What's your character's greatest fear?
12. Is your character an optimist or a pessimist? Does he have a sense of humor?
13. According to your character, what's her worst flaw?
14. What's his biggest flaw according to people who know him?

15. With what animals does your character identify?

16. With what animals does your character live?

17. What does your character do for fun or recreation?

18. What's your character's e-mail address?

19. What are your character's favorite Web sites?

20. What does your character usually bring to potluck dinners?

21. Does your character have any tattoos? If so, what and where?

22. What other details do you know about your character?

You may laugh at some of these questions (e-mail address? potluck dinners? tattoos?), but each of them helps you create more fully developed characters in a distinctive way. For example, a character whose e-mail address is keepontruckin@haha.com will be quite different from the character whose e-ddress is jpharrisonesq@harrisonandharrisonlaw.org.

The other wonderful thing about this exercise is that the characters who grow from it will be products of your imagination rather than copies of people you know. Even if a character begins as someone you know, you can't know some of these details about that person (in fact, you can't know everything about any real person, including, I would argue, yourself), so you will have to make them up. That's a good thing, first of all because it helps you stretch your fiction muscles and see what they can do, and second because fictitious people are almost always more interesting than real ones.

Finally, as E.M. Forster pointed out in *Aspects of the Novel*, "In daily life we never understand each other ... but people in a novel can be understood completely by the reader." This observation also reminds us why we're attracted to fiction in the first place.

DO I DO THIS FOR ALL MY CHARACTERS?

I'm often asked this question, and I used to insist that I didn't do it at all. That's because my characters seem to arrive fully developed, like Aphrodite on her half shell. But while this *is* true for me, I've come to realize that my original answer was disingenuous. The truth is I simply create my characters differently; the character development I'm suggesting you do on paper instead takes place in my right brain—at the same time those fictional seeds are germinating.

So my revised answer to this question is yes, I *do* do this for all my characters, not just my protagonist. In fact, even the walk-ons in my fiction arrive with ages, attitudes, and passions, and I know a great deal more than these basic facts about my main characters. Not all of this information will make its way into a fiction, but I believe that, as the author, it's my responsibility to know everything about the people who live there.

Incorporate Your Information

The second important aspect of creating characters is the *way* you incorporate what you know about them into your fiction. As Macauley and Lanning note in *Technique in Fiction*, in nineteenth-century novels, every time a new character appears, he shows up with his complete biography, not to mention his standing in society and what others think of him. Here is an example from George Eliot's novel *Adam Bede*:

> It is clear that the next workman is Adam's brother. He is nearly as tall; he has the same type of features, the same hue of hair and complexion; but the strength of the family likeness seems only to render more conspicuous the remarkable difference of expression both in form and face. Seth's

broad shoulders have a slight stoop; his eyes are grey; his eyebrows have less prominence and more repose than his brother's ...

What do you know about Seth from this paragraph? Well, he's tall and he looks like his brother Adam, though there's a "remarkable difference of expression both in form and face." But what else do you know? The answer is that all we have here is a lengthy description of Seth's appearance. And is Seth someone your reader cares about? Not yet. And maybe, not ever.

CLUES TO CHARACTER

Twenty-first-century readers (that's us!) neither want nor expect these lengthy introductions. As Noah Lukeman points out in *The Plot Thickens*, "Something as minor as a character trait can actually influence—in some cases, even define—the plot." In fact, because we're immersed in the nuances of psychology (even if we've never taken Psych 101), we can intuit a great deal about a character from one small bit of information. So rather than lengthy introductions like the one above, we get character "on the run."

What I mean by this is that character (along with setting, plot, point of view, and even a dash of foreshadowing) are all dropped into the fiction while the narrative continues to move forward. Here's an example from early in my own novel *Dissonance*. This paragraph introduces one of the main characters, Hana Weissova, to the reader. I've emphasized the "clues."

> **She was worried** about **Heidi's** chicken pox. She **knew it was foolish**; she hadn't worried about **Pavel's**, but he seemed so much sturdier than **his baby sister**, and always had. She **sat up through the night next to the baby's crib, listening to Bartók turned down low on the radio set,** and to **the occasional news reports that interrupted the music.** It seemed certain that **the British were going to hand**

Czechoslovakia to Hitler, that dreadful man. To **Hana**, it made no sense: Czechoslovakia was not England's to give.

Lots of clues, huh? What do you know about Hana from this paragraph? Here are the things I, the author, want you to know:

- Hana has two children: a son, Pavel, and a baby daughter, Heidi.
- Hana is a typically devoted and concerned mother.
- The time period is just before World War II.
- Hana is the kind of person who listens to Bartók.
- Hana lives in Czechoslovakia.
- Hana is starting to worry about Hitler.

If you formed an opinion as to whether or not you care about Hana from this paragraph, I've succeeded on another level, as well: In one brief paragraph, I've created a character to whom you've had as real a response as if you'd actually met her. In fact, you have!

What you need to remember is that, as the author, you have a responsibility to know every aspect of your character's biography. How much of that biography you share with your readers will ultimately depend on the story you're telling.

THE SPECIFIC DISTINCTIVE TRAIT

Whether you're dealing with just a few characters or a cast of thousands, creating what I call a "specific distinctive trait" for each will help your readers remember who each character is without you having to remind them in narrative. This means that instead of writing "Jean's sister Emma" whenever Emma appears on the scene, you can instead illustrate something about Emma that readers already know to jog their memories.

Perhaps my favorite example of a writer employing this method occurs in Susan Minot's *Evening*. Because most of this novel unfolds at a wedding, it includes an ensemble of characters. Minot helps readers remember who's who by "tagging" each character with something that will remind readers of that character's specific distinctive trait.

This approach allows Minot to place five or even ten characters in one scene without the reader losing track. To illustrate, here are two of the characters in two different scenes. In the first excerpt, we meet these characters for the first time.

> The [car] doors were open and she saw in front Buddy Wittenborn and in the driver's seat Ralph Eastman …. When she got close Ralph caught sight of her and jumped out of the car and Buddy looked over with a lazy smile.

This second excerpt takes place the morning of the wedding about halfway through the book.

Pacing down near the pink mallow was Ralph Eastman holding a piece of paper, gesturing with his hands, practicing his toast …. When she came out of the trees she found the small round lawn occupied by Buddy Wittenborn lying asleep on his back with his bare feet crossed and with his hands folded on his chest ….

What can you deduce about Ralph Eastman and Buddy Wittenborn from these brief selections? Do you see how using a specific distinctive trait "on the run" helps you "see" a character?

THE TELLING DETAIL

This brings us to one of my favorite aspects of character, the telling detail. E.M. Forster notes that a novelist "may not choose to tell us all he knows—many of the facts, even of the kind we call obvious, may be hidden." Beginning (and some not-so-beginning) writers often feel as if they must give every detail about a character, but if you do this, not only will your reader be frustrated, he *still* won't see what's in *your* head. I'm not saying you shouldn't note everything in your first draft—after all, a first draft is a wonderful way to find out what you're trying to say. Ultimately, though, it's the telling detail, and only the telling detail, that you'll want to hang on to. I've co-opted the Greek term *synecdoche* (sin-NEK-toe-kee), a linguistic term that means the part stands for the whole ("bread" for food; "soldier" for army), to represent how the right telling detail insists the reader fill in what he doesn't know. A good telling detail performs double—no, triple—duty, revealing setting, character, and plot all in one tidy line.

For an example of how this works, let's get in someone else's car. No, wait—we can't get in, not yet, because first we have to pick up the various books and papers on the passenger seat and toss them in the back. Okay, now we can slide in …. But, no: Now we see that the footwell has become the resting place for fast-food soft-drink cups, crumpled napkins, CD covers, even a hairbrush.

Okay. What do you know about the driver of this car from what I've just told you? The answer is that each of you will have conjured a different car and a different driver based on your—you guessed it—resources of experience.

GETTING INSIDE YOUR READER'S HEAD

My attempts to explain how a telling detail leads the reader to fill in what he doesn't know were made much simpler the first time I drew the following on a whiteboard:

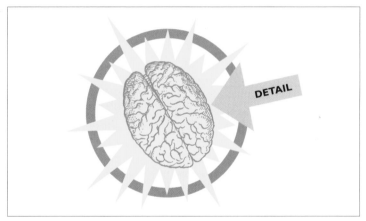

Imagine the circle is your reader's brain. When the right detail (the arrow) breaks through, it will explode in your reader's head so he fills in all sorts of details you haven't shown.

In a successful synecdoche, every reader will imagine a different picture of that car based on the telling details you choose to reveal. This is a good thing, because it means you've captured your readers' imaginations. It's also why, when we readers go to the movies, we're almost never as happy with the film as we were with the book. Unless the character the director imagines segues perfectly with our own picture (an astronomical unlikelihood), we're destined to be disappointed.

I'll talk more about the telling detail, synecdoche, and their relationship to setting in chapter four.

Let's Go to the Movies

Years ago, in his long-neglected *Novels Into Film*, George Bluestone noted the essential difference between the film and the novel: "One may ... see visually through the eye or imaginatively through the mind." Bluestone calls what happens when we read *persistence of vision*: "The eye fills in the gaps [so that] one may see visually through the eye [e.g., in films] or imaginatively through the mind [as we do when we read]."

What this means is that we experience film in a very different way than we do fiction—or, for that matter, anything we read. Viewing a film is a passive activity in which we receive information via sight (and sound). Reading, on the other hand, is active because we receive the information in a format that must be translated by the mind.

This goes a long way toward explaining why some of us prefer commercial fiction and others prefer more literary works. Because the former is plot driven while the latter is character driven, those of us who like action will want narratives whose plot drives the characters, while those who want to work a bit (or a lot) harder will look for narratives where characters drive the plot.

WHO'S PLAYING WHOM?

Quite a number of writers I know cast their fictions, either before they begin or at some point while they're writing. This ploy seems especially helpful to writers who can't seem to get a clear picture of their characters in their heads. One writer I know goes so far as to cut photos of film stars from celebrity magazines, write her characters' names below each photo, and pin them to her bulletin board.

When I first began touring for my novel *Dissonance*, a lot of questions took me by surprise. I'd expected to be asked how I came up with the metaphor of dissonance, or how I made a connection between music theory, the World War II concentration camp Terezín, and Los Alamos, New Mexico (hint: three seeds). Instead, I was asked if I wrote longhand or with a computer (answer: both), if I was a pianist (no, I'm not), and who I hoped would be cast in the film version.

This last question afforded me an opportunity to daydream about the Academy Award I'd win for the film adaptation (and the gorgeous gown I'd be wearing when I accepted it), and of course how, when I accepted it, I'd invite the actors onto the stage with me. That's when Meryl Streep and Julianna Margulies showed up. It turned out I'd cast my novel without even realizing it!

MINDING YOUR STORY
Character Walks Into a Room

How do you codify the information you receive? Think about it: So much information comes our way every day that we have to have some way of quickly deciding what goes where. When it comes to people, you may use a method you're not even aware of, such as the Myers-Briggs personality-type indicator, astrological signs, or even ethnic or racial stereotypes. We all need such systems, though we don't always share them with others.

Whenever my dear friend Joanie walks into a restaurant, she immediately looks around the room to see who she knows, then stops to visit with each person. However, when I walk into that restaurant (with her, let's say), I take in the whole room—what it looks and feels like, how many people are there, if it's smoky, if it's hot or cold. Then, as quickly as I can without drawing attention to myself (because the last thing a writer wants is to draw attention to herself), I find a quiet corner where I can watch everyone. My husband Bob, meanwhile, will examine the construction materials, while another friend will likely already have noted what could stand improvement.

Quick now, before you think about it, what do you know about the four people I've just described entering this restaurant? This exercise combines almost everything we've discussed in this chapter: what you know about your character, the telling detail, and the specific distinctive trait.

Now it's your turn. Walk into that restaurant yourself. What's the first thing you notice? How about your partner? What does he or she see? Try it out with a few friends. (I've asked quite a few of mine since I came up with this, and I'm always surprised by their answers.)

Then, have a character walk into a restaurant. What does she notice? What does she miss? And where in the restaurant does she head as soon as she can?

What have you learned about your character from this exercise? It may well be just the telling detail your fiction needs.

chapter 3
THE PLOT THICKENS

If you've ever asked a child about his day in school, you've likely already encountered the difference between story and plot. "The school bus came," the child's story begins, and then proceeds in a linear fashion through his day. Even if something unusual or exciting happened—at lunch, say—in the child's version, you won't hear about it until the linear retelling arrives at lunchtime.

If, on the other hand, you ask a high school student about her day, she'll likely begin (after shrugging her shoulders and saying "fine" at first) with that day's highlight: "During biology, Donnie Bakeless let the frogs loose. We ran all over the room, and then out into the hall, trying to catch them."

The difference between these two tellings is that the older child has learned to apply plot to a story in order to make it more interesting to the listener (or reader). She's skipped the boring parts (such as the bus ride and Pledge of Allegiance the younger child will relate in his linear telling) and found an amusing highlight, then *arranged* that highlight's placement. Finally, without even being aware she's doing so, she "tells" that plot so it "reads" better.

Elements of Plot

Like all humans, you already know how to arrange events in this way.

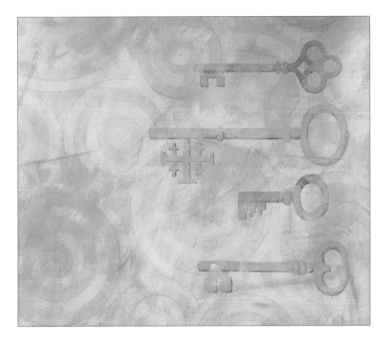

The key lies in understanding what E.M. Forster calls "the fundamental difference between story and plot." No one has better explained this than Forster in *Aspects of the Novel*, so if you need to learn plot basics, studying this primary source will serve you far better than any reiteration I could provide. Forster tells us that the main difference between story and plot is that plot has the added element of causality: This happened *because* this happened, rather than a "this happened, then that happened" recitation like the child's on the previous page.

But *great* plotting requires more than mere causality: It needs forward motion, action (whether exterior or interior), and most importantly, conflict. A good plot not only grabs a reader from the first page and doesn't let him go until the last page is turned, it also leaves him feeling as if the journey was well worth the time he spent taking it. That's because within every great plot are lots of little plots, some of which are introduced and concluded within one scene and some of which come and go throughout the length of the fiction.

Finally, the best plots are intertwined with every other aspect of fiction, from intriguing seeds and compelling characters to accurate pacing and distinctive voice. But enough summary statement—let's get into the plot of *this* chapter.

But George Was Curious ...

The key to forward momentum lies in that basic element of human nature, curiosity: Once we've glimpsed the edge of something, we can't help but want to see the whole thing. Still stronger temptations to our curiosity are things like the secret door we're told we can't open or the mysterious stranger who rides into town. Whatever we don't know—especially if we're told we *can't* or *shouldn't* know it—we want to know. In fiction (as in real life), questions beget questions, some of which are answered quickly and some of which take an entire novel to unfold.

In early drafts of novels, writers often ask and answer one question at a time, plodding from chapter to chapter until every question has been answered and they type "The End." But some of these questions are far bigger than others, and the bigger the question, the more emotional weight it can carry.

When I come across one of these bigger questions in a student's manuscript, I'll ask the author why it was dropped so quickly. Why not, I'll suggest, drag it out a little longer, or even, if it's particularly compelling, for most of the length of the novel? Still more importantly, it will sometimes seem to me as if one of these chapter-long questions (and its answer) is the heart of the novel and should, in fact, be its biggest question.

This often happens when we begin with what we think is a big question, only to be diverted by something still bigger in the writing of it. Being open and alert to these bigger questions is the equivalent of unwrapping gifts from your unconscious.

SO, WHAT'S YOUR QUESTION?

Quite simply, the biggest question is the one with which you'll begin and end your fiction. It will create your story arc, which will look like this:

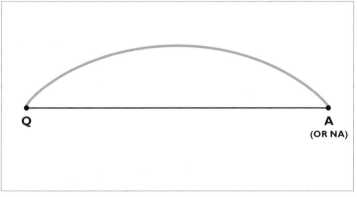

A novel's biggest question begins at its inception and is answered (or not answered) at its conclusion.

I like to think of this broadest story arc as the fiction's umbrella. All its other questions will lie beneath this umbrella, so that not only the entire fiction but also each chapter and scene will have its events arranged with questions—and some answers—at each turn. Let's add these smaller arcs to the diagram above:

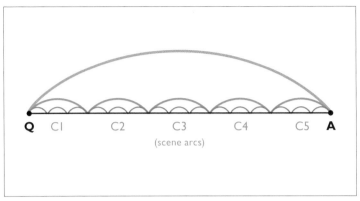

Every chapter and every scene has an arc as well.

But still other questions are not resolved within a scene or chapter. Some—let's call them the song-and-dance teams, after the supporting cast members of Broadway musicals—will have a plot of their own that will serve to reinforce the main plot. That story arc will look like this on our main diagram:

Subplots reinforce the main plot.

Finally, there are the questions that begin and end according to their own particular weights. Bigger questions will come back again and again before being answered at the end of their arcs, while smaller questions will pop up and just as quickly be gone. Our umbrella plot arc diagram, with every type question and answer included, will ultimately end up looking something like this:

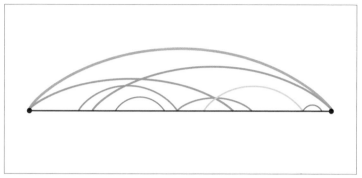

Each story arc takes up as much weight as it requires beneath the main umbrella.

OH, WHAT A BEAUTIFUL MORNING

Yikes! For a relatively straightforward example, let's turn to one of those Broadway musicals I just mentioned, *Oklahoma!* The main plot of *Oklahoma!* concerns Curly and Laurey; the musical opens with Curly asking Laurey to go to the barn raising with him and ends with Curly and Laurey's wedding $(x \to y)$. Shortly after we meet Curly and Laurey, we meet Ado Annie and Will, the song-and-dance team whose courtship's often amusing ups-and-downs serve as a supporting subplot to the main plot $(a \to b)$.

But other questions and answers come and go. There's the traveling salesman who recognizes Ado Annie as "a girl who caint say no" $(c \to d)$; the slow-witted Jud, who either loves or lusts after Laurey, depending on who's interpreting the script $(e \to f)$; and the conflicts between farmers and cowhands $(g \to h)$. Each of these smaller story arcs can be drawn beneath the larger umbrella of the main plot like this:

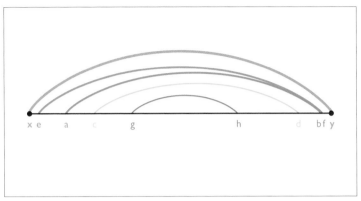

The main plot and subplots of *Oklahoma!*

Even if you're not familiar with this particular Broadway musical, you can see how the subplots both stand alone and reinforce the larger plot. Remember: The end of each arc represents a question answered. Whether to dangle the question as long as possible—as in whether Ado Annie will marry Will or the traveling salesman $(a \to b)$—or open and shut it quickly—as in the feud between farmers and cowhands $(g \to h)$—is determined by the importance of the question to your larger plot.

Lisa's Surefire, All-Inclusive Plot Formula

There are as many plot formulae (or possibly more) as there are books about writing. I've found that the simpler one can make an idea, the easier it is to grasp. So here's my surefire, all-inclusive, every-plot-looks-like-this formula:

1. Someone wants something.
2. Something or someone else stands in Someone's way.
3. Someone does or doesn't get what Someone wants.

To see how this works, let's apply this formula to *Oklahoma!*:

1. Curly wants Laurey.
2. Jud wants Laurey, too.
3. Curly gets Laurey.

Too simple? Let's apply it to something more complicated, like Harper Lee's *To Kill a Mockingbird*:

1. Atticus Finch wants justice for the wrongly accused Tom Robinson.
2. Mayella Ewell and her father, Bob Ewell, stand in his way.
3. Justice ultimately prevails, though not in the way anyone might have expected, least of all Atticus Finch.

That "though," by the way, signals a plot that will ultimately prove far more satisfying than a simpler one like that of *Oklahoma!*

Try applying this formula to the plots of some books you've read recently. Or try it out on a film or two. And, if you can't wait, skip to the end of this chapter, where an exercise will show you how to apply it to your own fiction.

Keep It Moving

The next aspect of plot to keep in mind is forward momentum. Your story begins here and continues on to here:

Your story begins at *X* and continues to its conclusion at *Y*.

That *X*—that beginning—answers the question, "Why now?" Why, for example, does Kafka's "The Metamorphosis" begin at the moment it does? Because it's the moment Gregor Samsa awakes to find he's turned into a giant bug. J.D. Salinger's *The Catcher in the Rye* opens with a sly reference to "that David Copperfield kind of crap" before beginning with "the day I left Pencey Prep," which is the moment Holden Caulfield's angst reaches crisis proportions for reasons the reader will discover as the plot progresses.

Where does your fiction begin? Do you have some of that "David Copperfield kind of crap" going on before your forward momentum begins? If so, you'll want to rethink a bit, because from your beginning, *X*, your fiction should begin to move forward.

RISING ACTION

If you break your fiction into roughly four equal sections, something major will occur at roughly each section shift: one-quarter of the way through, halfway, and at the three-quarter mark. I draw it like this:

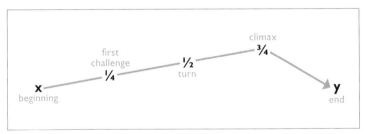

From its beginning, your fiction's action rises, its oppositions deepen, and its conflicts escalate, to the first challenge (¼), the turn (½), and finally, the climax (¾). The denouement then takes the reader to the fiction's end, leaving him feeling both satisfied and fulfilled.

To do this with your own fiction, begin by imagining your narrative divided into four roughly equal sections. If you have a twenty-page short story, for example, each section will be five pages long. How you arrange the events that happen in each section will add up to your fiction's plot trajectory. It won't necessarily be linear. (Witness Alice Munro's short stories.) It won't necessarily cover every moment. (In fact, it shouldn't.) But it should include each of the following:

1. You begin. In the first section, you'll ask the "what if?" that's at the heart of your narrative. Your reader will discover what's at stake for your protagonist as you introduce the oppositions that begin your narrative's forward motion. There are as many kinds of oppositions as there are stories. Yours may involve—to name but a few—conflict, doubt, struggle, or rivalry, and may be internal or external. You have one-fourth of your narrative to set this opposition up. At the one-quarter mark, it will rear its ugly little head in some substantive way.

2. The action rises, the oppositions deepen, and the conflicts escalate. Once your oppositions have been established, you'll begin to deepen them. This is what's called *rising action*, and it will take us through the midpoint of your narrative, where there will be a shift toward more rapid movement. At the halfway point, a big shift will occur. It won't be the climax but some turning point.

I've said this so many times, so authoritatively, that I thought I had better go back and check my own work. Here are a few examples of what I found: A wedding. A revelation. A confession. An arrival. A new character. None of these are the climactic moment. But they do increase the momentum toward that climax.

3. The momentum builds more quickly as it approaches the climax. By this third quadrant, so inexorable are the forces at work that the reader should feel as if she is being pulled along by a current. That's because we're heading for the crisis, the flash point at which your narrative turns. This will occur approximately three-quarters through your narrative. It may happen with a bang or a whimper, but it should be a clear turning point for your plot—and your protagonist.

4. And they lived happily ever after. Or not. Finally, your narrative will have a resolution. If you've ever read a book that seems rushed at the end, it's because many authors are so relieved to have gotten to their climax, they rush through what comes after it. (I like to call the denouement the cigarette, though this analogy has become something of an anachronism.) Rushing to the finish after the climax is a mistake: Our human need for storytelling requires closure as much as it requires the story itself. A satisfying narrative is one where the reader is left feeling not only that the ending was inevitable, but that he—and the author—enjoyed every moment it took to arrive there. If you rush to the finish, the reader may be left feeling cheated, no matter how good he was feeling up until then.

UPPING THE ANTE

Reader anticipation increases relative to character anticipation because, as Noah Lukeman points out in *The Plot Thickens*, "Suspense, ultimately, is about anticipation. It is about what we do *not* have, what has *not* happened."

Prolonging anticipation becomes second nature once you think about what's at stake. If the outcome of the trial will change everything one way or the other, for example, you'll want to postpone the verdict as long as you can. Or, if your character's next move hinges on someone else's decision, anticipation will increase if you make that person unavailable or, better still, have her disappear without explanation. One more example should suffice before we move on: If the protagonist doesn't realize it's a wolf at her door, she may first wonder at the size of the wolf's eyes, ears, and teeth before we arrive at the story's climax.

THE MOST IMPORTANT THING YOUR PLOT WILL EVER DO

Picture your reader reading your book. You've caught her attention. She never looks up. She turns page after page. The most important thing you'll do for her is keep your fiction moving forward.

Uh-oh: She's beginning to fidget. She adjusts her position. But she still can't put your book down. That's good. It's possible she needs to take a break, perhaps to use the bathroom. No, she's still reading, but ultimately, one of two things will occur. (1) Your reader will become more and more physically uncomfortable as she continues reading; finally, she'll get up and walk to the bathroom—taking your book with her, or (2) your reader will come to the end of a chapter, or a line break, or some point where she feels she can stop, and she'll put the book down before she goes to the bathroom.

Which of these scenarios is preferable? Why, the first, of course. You want your reader to keep reading. And the way you do that is to keep her curiosity piqued—keep enough questions unanswered that she'll continue reading to find their answers, meanwhile answering enough smaller questions to keep her satisfied. You want your reader to keep reading past her bedtime, on her breaks, every chance she gets. You've read that book yourself. Now you're going to write it!

MINDING YOUR STORY
Who Wants What?

Earlier in this chapter, I asked you to apply my all-purpose plot formula to a few books and films. Now it's time to take that exercise one step further and apply it to a fiction of your own.

Pick a fiction you know isn't yet in its final form. Now, very quickly, answer these three questions:

1. Who wants what?
2. Who or what stands in his/her way?
3. Does s/he get what s/he wants?

Were you able to answer these questions one, two, three? Did you struggle with number two or with number three? If you did, I'd suggest you list all of the questions and answers throughout your fiction. Now, with which of these questions does your fiction currently begin? Is it the biggest question? If it's not, which is? Can you answer the three questions above with *that* as your biggest question? Or, can you imagine answering them?

So much of what we write begins with the seed of one idea, but for that idea to fully flower it must be cross-pollinated with many others as well. If you've ever begun with a flurry of rapid writing and then suddenly petered out, you've learned what happens if you start too soon. Or, if you've kept doggedly at it, only to arrive at the end knowing something is missing, or somewhere in the middle knowing you've made a wrong turn, you've learned what happens when you push a one-trick pony too far.

Working with the questions and answers that make up your plot to uncover the biggest question can provide new energy to fiction that has been languishing in your closet. Don't be afraid to start over. It's often where the best fiction begins.

chapter 4
WHERE IT'S AT

Does it matter where your story unfolds? Not only is the answer *yes*, it's true in far more ways than you may have previously considered. It matters, for example, if you want to use your setting to help reveal your characters and plot. Think about what Hogwarts reveals about Harry Potter and his friends and their story, what Africa reveals about *The Poisonwood Bible*'s multiple narrators and their stories, even what a largely unnamed suburbia reveals for Rick Moody's or Ann Beattie's characters and plots. And it also matters if you want to make an immediate connection with your reader, immersing her at once in your fiction's particular universe.

In fact, the term "setting" encompasses far more than the place a fiction unfolds; it establishes a fiction's mood, feeling, and historical era. In addition, setting is tied to a fiction's point of view—so much so that until point of view has been firmly established, the setting can't really be distinctly rendered. Of course, while the term *point of view* refers only to sight, the strongest settings are created by using all of the senses (even—or especially—the sixth).

Last but not least, your fiction's setting offers it—and you, its author—credence, by way of its veracity. In other words, the truer your setting is, the more believable the fictional world you invite your reader to enter.

In this chapter, we'll explore how a variety of masters create settings that do all these things, and more, while remaining true to their particular fictions' worlds.

The Vivid Palette

One of the toughest aspects of creating a setting is making a fictive milieu vivid to the reader. Consider these two descriptions of the view out my office window (which, in my defense, I've made up just this minute):

1. The rugged Sandia Mountains are a beautiful backdrop to the growing southwestern city.

2. Rising two-dimensionally from the eastern foothills, the ever-changing rocky face of the Sandias forces the city to an abrupt end. Sunsets briefly paint the mountains a watermelon pink, a color that lent them their Spanish name, but the mountains change from moment to moment in the aching clarity of desert light.

In the first example, I used (as best I could) vague descriptive adjectives, which do nothing to differentiate these particular mountains from any others, and a do-nothing verb, "are." In the second, I tried to use far more concrete verbs and adjectives in order (I hope) to draw these mountains in far more particularity.

MATCH YOUR DETAILS TO YOUR FICTION

Another aspect of creating a vivid palette is choosing details that are right for this *particular* fiction. Here, for example, is Scout Finch in the opening pages of Harper Lee's classic *To Kill a Mockingbird*:

> Maycomb was an old town, but it was a tired old town when I first knew it. In rainy weather the streets turned to red slop; grass grew on the sidewalks, the courthouse sagged in the square. Somehow, it was hotter, then: a black dog suffered on a summer's day; bony mules hitched to Hoover carts flicked flies in the sweltering shade of the live oaks on the

square. Men's stiff collars wilted by nine in the morning. Ladies bathed before noon, after their three-o'clock naps, and by nightfall were like soft teacakes with frostings of sweat and sweet talcum.

In this brief paragraph, Lee sets the stage for all that follows by employing the classic (dare I use the word?) formula for setting:

+ accuracy
+ originality
+ the telling detail

Let's look at each of these three items individually. First, accuracy: The particularity of the details Lee chooses lends the novel a credence that feels "true" to the reader. Second, originality: Look at how Lee describes the rainy streets: They "turned to red slop." Or, the verb she chooses to describe the men's "stiff collars": They "*wilted* by nine in morning."

More striking, however, are the details themselves, which in their distinct originality show us not only the heat but how this *specific* heat affects the people (and, in this case, the animals) in this town; for example, those ladies who "by nightfall were like soft teacakes with frostings of sweat and sweet talcum."

This is an especially perfect detail because it not only describes the ladies and the town but also shows us something else about the town at the same time—that this is the kind of place where such teacakes might be served. In fact, the best details will always relate to the greater whole, or, to put it another way, they'll *belong* in a particular story. If Lee had used, say, Saharan Desert imagery to describe her Maycomb, not only would the reader be confused, the author wouldn't have fulfilled the secondary purpose of using setting to reveal character and plot. But because Lee uses details that belong in *this* story, this paragraph moves far beyond the usual visual description. We *feel* the sagging courthouse, *smell* the mules flicking flies, and can almost *taste* those wilting collars and those ladies like soft teacakes.

Finally, in addition to drawing us a vivid portrait of this sleepy southern town, this marvelous paragraph tells us some important things about its narrator as well. First, she's a reminiscent narrator. We are clued in to this because of phrases such as "when I first knew it" and "it was hotter, then." A reminiscent narrator will have the advantage of hindsight when looking back at her story, as the now-grown Scout does. Secondly, we learn that our narrator is curious, that she notices things and then reports them. This will become more and more important as the story unfolds.

The Part Is the Whole

Master short story writer and playwright Anton Chekhov wrote, "Snatch at *small* details, grouping them in such a manner that after reading them, one can obtain the picture on closing one's eyes." Consider the small details in Harper Lee's paragraph above. With just the few details Lee provides, the reader can sketch in an entire town.

You may recall from chapter two the Greek term *synecdoche*, which refers to a linguistic trope whereby a part is used to stand for a whole, and the fact that I like to use this term to refer to the ability of the human mind to take one detail and create a character. Here, we can apply the same concept to scene. In the scene above, Lee uses telling details that describe the sidewalks, courthouse, live oaks, and town square to anchor the picture her reader forms of Maycomb.

The ability to create a whole from a part is an interesting aspect of the human mind. In fact, I can throw just about any telling detail at you and you will form a complete picture in your head. When I first introduced this concept in chapter two, I talked about finding the right detail to reveal a character. When it comes to setting, though, this tool goes further still.

THE BIG PICTURE BLOSSOMS

Let's try this with a few other details to see how it works. There's the classic example from J.D. Salinger's *The Catcher in the Rye* (cited by Macauley and Lanning in *Technique in Fiction*): "The lobby smelled ... like fifty million dead cigars." Can you see that lobby, even though Salinger offers only its scent? Or, there's this, from Judith Freeman's *Red Water* (the point-of-view character is on horseback):

> Leaving the settlement, she took a trail through an open field where a herd of slat-ribbed cows had bedded down to wait out the heat of the day. They sat chewing their cuds, then scrambled to their feet as she passed by and stood looking at her with their legs splayed, gazing out with fearful eyes.

Not only do we see this open field of cows, we see these particular "slat-ribbed" cows and the way they stare at the protagonist as she rides past. That's what I mean by picking just the right detail: We see not just the scene but the character(s) in it and the plot moving forward.

While it's every writer's desire that our readers see precisely the picture we've got in our heads, in reality this is impossible given the medium we're using: All we have is words to draw our pictures. That's what's wonderful about synecdoche; the right word, the right telling detail, will blossom in the reader's brain to form a complete picture. It won't be our picture, but that's okay. Because the reader imagined it, it will be all the more vivid for him. Remember that diagram from chapter two? It applies here as well.

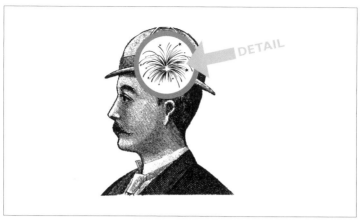

The right telling detail will penetrate your reader's brain and explode into a full picture.

More Than a Feeling

As surely as the weather, setting creates a fiction's mood. The first paragraph of *To Kill a Mockingbird* lets us know this novel will be full of slow, hot days, during which even the slightest of movements will take some effort. A different fiction, however, will begin with a different setting, as does Raymond Chandler's first novel, *The Big Sleep*:

> It was about eleven o'clock in the morning, mid-October, with the sun not shining and a look of hard wet rain in the clearness of the foothills. I was wearing my powder-blue suit, with dark blue shirt, tie, and display handkerchief, black brogues, black wool socks with dark blue clocks on them. I was neat, clean, shaved, and sober, and I didn't care who knew it. I was everything the well-dressed private detective ought to be. I was calling on four million dollars.

"Now, wait!" you might be saying. "That's a whole lot about what he's wearing and only one bit of setting!" I'm using Chandler as an example largely because of that objection. Chandler, like most seasoned writers, mixes all his fictive techniques together. So while it may seem like we're getting Marlowe's wardrobe of the day, we're also getting the time (eleven o'clock, mid-October); the weather; Marlowe's voice, character, and point of view; and the setting (Marlowe's "calling on four million dollars"). It tells us everything we need to know about where we are.

Of course, in the next paragraph, we get a lot more detail on what "four million dollars" looks like. The paragraph begins, "The main hallway of the Sternwood place was two stories high," and continues on to describe a stained-glass panel over the entrance doors in great detail before moving on to the outdoors visible at the back of the hall. Here, too, Chandler can't help but give us voice, character, and point of view: "Beyond the garage were some decorative trees trimmed as carefully as poodle dogs."

I can see those trees; can you? In fact, I can picture everything about the Sternwood place, just from the details Chandler provides. This is because we see it through Marlowe's cynical eyes and hear his jaded voice telling us what he sees. In this way, the contrast between his internal and external environments sets the mood. The best telling detail acquires a sort of guilt by association, in this case, the "hard wet rain" of an L.A. October and the voice of a "well-dressed private detective."

SETTING AS MYSTERY

Even if you're not writing a mystery, you can establish questions in a reader's mind via your setting. Here's a brief example from my short story "Wild Horses," which I first cited in chapter one, and which appears in appendix A.

> Neighbors watched for her little pickup along the county road. Sometimes Althea would pull over, or not pull over, and stop. Janet Kendall once found her

sitting on her tailgate in the middle of the road just over a rise, had slammed on her brakes and skidded to a dusty halt just short of the rear bumper.

This section appears fairly early in the story, and, while it's clear from the outset that something's not quite right with Althea, we don't yet know what's wrong with her. This brief scene, which further establishes the story's southwest Colorado milieu, at the same time adds to the reader's curiosity about what's wrong with Althea.

SETTING AS COMFORT ZONE

Still another way of using setting to convey mood is by creating a sense of comfort. This can go two ways, of course. Consider just about anything written by Stephen King, who lulls the reader into a false sense of security by the very everydayness of his opening settings. Or, read again the opening of *To Kill a Mockingbird*, which practically rocks us to sleep with its familiar, slow, hot summer afternoon.

Setting the Clock

Still another thing both Lee and Chandler are doing via their chosen details is establishing the historical period, Lee with her powdered ladies and Chandler with his dressed-to-the-nines private investigator. Details in settings are like clues, and the astute reader will learn more about a fiction's time period from the right details than from a tidy header that reads, "Los Angeles, California, 1939."

Here's another example, again from Judith Freeman's *Red Water*:

We landed at the port of Boston and traveled across country by train, in boxcars fitted out with special seats, reaching Iowa City on July 5th.

> With the help of the Perpetual Emigrating Fund, which advanced us much-needed money for our journey, we were able to secure a place with the Willy Handcart Company, and although it was late in the year to begin the crossing of the plains, our party was anxious to set out, for nothing less than Zion awaited us in the mountains to the west.

Notice how this selection establishes voice (via its nineteenth-century phrasings) and mood (anticipation, fear, and longing) as well as its historical period. In fact, the voice is part of what clues us in to the time period. Contemporary settings are similarly immediately recognizable to a reader, as in this brief aside from Carol Shields's last novel, *Unless*:

> Emma Allen sent me an e-mail from Newfoundland yesterday. She and her daughter and her widowed daughter-in-law were off to a health spa for the weekend, she wrote ...

Just as the fact that Freeman's narrator must take a train across country alerts us to a nineteenth-century America, Shields's e-mail and health spa let us know we're in our own time and milieu.

One last thing to be aware of as you use setting to create a time: As you likely learned in high school, you need to beware of anachronisms in your fiction. Nothing pulls a reader out of your story's world faster than having a character check his wristwatch before they were invented or having a letter arrive by Pony Express after its demise.

The Importance of Veracity

Just as you need to tie your details to your time, you have a responsibility to establish the veracity of those details. Whether it's when Lake Erie freezes in winter or the way the landlady of an Omaha boardinghouse might phrase something, it's up to you to make sure you get every last detail right. As I mentioned in this chapter's opening, the truer your setting, the more believable the fictional world you invite your reader to enter.

My favorite example of a fiction's lack of veracity comes from a short story I was once reading in a literary journal to remain unnamed. I was rather enjoying this story about a young man in Los Angeles for whom nothing was going right. Finally, the young man got in his car. He started driving. He drove east, across the desert. He drove and drove. He didn't stop until he reached Needles, Arizona.

Now, those of you not living in the American Southwest may not have noticed anything amiss. However, as anyone who's driven I-40 far too many times will tell you, Needles is not in Arizona. It's on the California side of the Colorado River.

For me, one reader, this author immediately lost his credibility. First of all, this lack of attention to a simple detail (didn't he have a Rand McNally, for heaven's sake?) told me I couldn't trust anything he told me. Second, the idea that he'd been so careless about a simple fact suggested a lack of attention to craft. But, most important of all, this negligence said the writer was writing about what he didn't know.

WRITING WHAT YOU DON'T KNOW

Unlike many writing teachers, I encourage writing about what you don't know. It's a great way to learn about things you might not have otherwise, and writing itself is a wonderful way of trying to understand people whose points of view are otherwise difficult for you to imagine. But with writing about what you don't know comes the responsibility of finding out. You can't make things up in fiction, not the things that matter. You can't write emotion falsely, and you can't get the details of a "real" setting wrong.

If the unnamed writer above had been writing science fiction, and if his story had been set in a futuristic American Southwest where the Colorado River's shifting (so that Needles was now, in fact, in Arizona rather than California) was an important part of the story, the detail he got wrong would instead have been something an alert reader would pick up on and note as one more example of a world gone awry. But because the only thing awry in this story was the writer's own compass, I put his story down without finishing it.

One View, One Point of View

The final key to making a setting vivid is to see it through one intense point of view. After all, if you want to make an immediate connection with your reader, you'll want to immerse her at once in your fiction's particular universe. In the next chapter, we'll be looking at point of view up close and personal. Even without that study, though, it's easy to see the difference between these two settings, the first from George Eliot's *Adam Bede* and the second from Carol Shields's *Unless*:

> 1. It is a very fine old place, of red brick, softened by a pale powdery lichen, which has dispersed itself with happy irregularity, so as to bring the red brick into terms of friendly companionship with the limestone ornaments surrounding the three gables, the windows, and the door-place ...

> 2. On a December morning I went walking hand in hand with Tom in the Orangetown cemetery ... The cold weather had broken, and the tops of the old limestone monuments, sun-plucked in their neat rows, were shiny with melting snow.

In the first example, Eliot reports the setting as if it were a gift from author to reader. Notice the vague adjectival clauses ("very fine"; "happy irregularity") and the lackluster verbs ("is"; "has"). Now compare this with the second brief example, from the vivid point of view of first-person narrator Reta Winters. Notice how we're looking at one thing, rows of gravestones, from one point of view. Even the limestone in the second selection appears clearer to the reader. Shields was a masterful writer (as was Eliot in her day), one who understood how the right verb (in this case, "sun-plucked") could do the work of three tired adjectives. But the lesson here goes further: When we see a setting through only one set of eyes, whether via first or third person, we see it far more clearly than we will when we view it from a distant omniscient point of view. Even when you're working in omniscient point of view, render physical detail through one character's eyes, and your reader will see your settings far more vividly.

The next time you're creating a setting, don't settle for the tried and trite. Make your setting work for you and for your fiction. Who knows? You could create the next *To Kill a Mockingbird*.

MINDING YOUR STORY
Using Your Senses

You've likely read (and written) many scenes that *show* everything there is to see about a place, real or imagined. But there are at least four other senses that can make your setting more vivid. (The sixth sense can also play a part, if you're comfortable using it.) As you create a scene, ask yourself the following questions:

- What can my characters hear?
- How does it feel?
- Can they taste it?

- Can they smell it?
- Can they sense it?

Smell and taste can be especially useful when you're setting a scene. Take, for example, Marcel Proust, who wrote volumes based on one bite into a madeleine. That's because smell and taste are tied to the limbic system, the oldest part of the brain, which triggers automatic responses such as "Woolly mammoth: Run like hell." For this reason, you can use smell or taste to trigger a character's memory just as it really happens for you and your reader.

But whether or not you choose to use a limbic sense to trigger a flashback, remembering to use more than sight to evoke a scene will make it all the more vivid to your reader. Just for fun, pick a scene you've already written and rewrite it using as many of your point-of-view character's senses as you can. You may not use every detail you uncover, but chances are you'll find more than one telling detail that will blossom in a reader's mind and draw the full picture for him.

chapter 5
WHAT'S YOUR POINT?

Let's pretend this is a classroom. I'll be the teacher. I'm sitting on the desk in the front of the room, facing the students seated in their tidy rows of desks. This is my point of view, and what and whom I see are very different from what my students (I'll call three of them Betty, Rob, and Debby) are seeing.

You there, Betty: You're in the front row. Not only do you see me sitting on the desk, you can see the words I've scribbled on the whiteboard behind me. From where he sits by the door, Rob can't see my face, only the hair that keeps falling over my eye as I talk. Over by the window, Debby's not looking at me at all; she's looking outside, where she sees the trees hanging listless on this hot July afternoon.

We may be in the same room, but each of us would tell the story of this particular moment in this particular classroom in a different way. I might write about the way each student is engaged or not engaged (see above). Betty might tell you what I'm wearing, the way I use my hands to emphasize my words, and what I said to her about her submission just before class began. Rob might focus on the fact that my hair keeps obscuring my face and what that says about me. And Debby, looking at those trees, might be remembering another summer, long ago and far away. Here we are, all in the same room at the same time, and yet, *depending on who's telling the story, there is a different story for each point of view.*

I can't see the whiteboard behind me, but my students can.

Whose Story Is It, Anyway?

If you're familiar with the classic Akira Kurosawa film *Rashomon*, you already know that a story can change dramatically depending on from whose point of view it's told. In *Rashomon*, something happens by the side of the road, and a man ends up dead. The highwayman accused of his murder tells one version of what happened. The man's wife relates a different version, while a woodcutter who happens on the scene tells still another. Finally, the dead man speaks through a medium, offering a fourth view of the events. Which version is true? It depends not only on what each person chooses to tell, but what he or she chooses *not* to tell.

Point of view assumes the trust implicit between speaker and listener. Until it's proven otherwise, a listener wants to believe the person telling a story, and the same is true of a reader and narrator. If you've ever listened to one side of a breakup story, not only do you know how a telling will be colored by point of view, you may also know how different the other person's version will be. The old adage, "There are two sides to every story," is only partly true. The reality is that there as many sides to a story as there are people who viewed it. And each will believe his version is the "true" one—because that's the way he saw it.

The main question to keep in mind as you consider point of view is, whose story is it, anyway? Each character will color what happened according to a number of factors. Point of view encompasses more than what a character can see, hear, smell, taste, feel, and sense; it also includes what a character *wants* someone else to know and what she'd rather we didn't see. But in fact, just as in real life, the more someone tries to color events a certain way, the more he ends up revealing not only about himself but about what really happened.

WHO WILL BE CHANGED?

One way to determine who will tell your story is to decide *who will be changed* by the events that unfold. Who, for example, is changed in *The Great Gatsby*? Well, yes, Gatsby's dead at the end of the novel, but his point of view has remained static. The character who has changed is Nick Carraway, the young narrator who tells us Gatsby's story. Same with *Moby-Dick*. Captain Ahab doesn't change (except that, as Gatsby, he dies). The whale doesn't change. Only Ishmael, our narrator, *has his worldview altered by the events that unfold.*

Look at these two examples another way. What kind of novel would *The Great Gatsby* be if it were told from Gatsby's point of view, or Daisy's? Gatsby might go on and on about unrequited love, while Daisy's narration would be a whirl of tennis, cocktails, and what-to-wear choices. If Captain Ahab told us *Moby-Dick*, we'd get all sorts of reasons that damned whale deserves to die, but with none of the narrative distance Ishmael offers us.

Pick a Point (of View)

Entire books have been written about point of view, and for good reason: No aspect of fiction writing determines your story's success or failure more. You can have terrific ideas, dynamic characters, a riveting plot, and compelling settings, but if the narrative is told from the wrong point of view (or points of view, which we'll get to in a moment), it can land on the page with a dull thud.

Point of view really comes down to one of just a few choices, each with its advantages and disadvantages. Let's look at each point of view possibility individually to help you begin to determine your own fiction's point.

LIMITED POINT OF VIEW

When a narrative is seen through one set of eyes, it is called a limited point of view. Whether first or third person (we'll discuss "person" in chapter six), limited point of view "sees" only what its point-of-view character sees. There are decided advantages to a limited point of view, not the least of which is the writer/reader bond of trust mentioned above. That bond establishes not just intimacy but identification, so the reader will root for the narrator no matter what horrid things the narrator perpetrates.

Another advantage of limited point of view is its sense of immediacy. For the reader, there's a sense of being "in" the story and a concurrent willingness to surrender herself to the fiction's demands.

But limited point of view, by its very nature, is "limited." The narrator can't see what's behind him (as I can't see the whiteboard behind me in the example that opened this chapter), nor can he know what's going on in other people's minds. A limited point-of-view narrator will always be unreliable because as soon as events are colored through one point of view, they are subjective rather than objective (although I'd argue there's no such thing as objectivity).

Finally, limited point of view demands that the narrator not withhold information for the sake of suspense. A dear departed friend once wrote a not-very-good mystery where, halfway through, the point-of-view character jetted off to the Caribbean, talked to a few people, and came back. It wasn't until the end of her narrative that the author revealed that the protagonist had discovered the clue that solved the mystery while she was gone.

I suggested my friend move her protagonist's trip closer to the climax of the book, but, not being a rewriter, she couldn't see how that was possible. I suggested someone back home supply the clue later on, but again, her book was "finished." I still smile when I think of this wonderful, stubborn friend and her equally stubborn narrator—along with her book, which could have been something if she'd wanted to invest more time in it.

CALL ME UNRELIABLE

It's possible, of course, to use an unreliable narrator to great advantage. In Mona Simpson's *Anywhere But Here*, we believe every awful thing Ann tells us about her mother, Adele, even though Ann tells us repeatedly she herself is a liar. Interestingly, Simpson challenges everything that came before with a six-page final chapter in which we hear from Adele herself, who tells us:

> It's the most important, beautiful, fulfilling thing I've ever done in my life, being a mother. And I look at her and think, Hey, I didn't do such a bad job. But she holds in her fear and her anger, she hasn't learned to let go yet …

Another example of the possibilities of an unreliable narrator can be found in William Styron's brilliant novel *Sophie's Choice*. While this novel is narrated by Stingo, the young outsider who, like Nick Carraway, will be forever changed by what he learns in his new foreign environment, Sophie narrates a series of sections in which she tells Stingo about her experiences during World War II.

But the story changes every time Sophie tells it. When we find out the terrible true story at the climax of the novel, we understand why she would make up so many false versions. These stories are as much for Sophie as they are for Stingo: She's trying to convince herself that she's not as bad as the truth makes her believe she is.

MULTIPLE-LIMITED OR SHIFTING POINT OF VIEW

Beginning writers love point of view so much that once they discover its possibilities, they can't wait to write from as many points of view as possible—all in the same fiction. "Why can't I?" they ask. The answer is that they can. (Of course, they can do anything they want, but that doesn't mean someone else will want to read their efforts if they do.)

Multiple-limited, also called shifting point of view, addresses some of the problems of limited point of view by moving from character to character. But multiple-limited point-of-view narratives set up difficulties that beginning (and often, more advanced) writers can't begin to surmount, in particular repetition, digression, and egregious omission.

REPETITION

When two (or more) characters are affected by a pivotal scene, it's natural to want to tell that scene from both points of view. But unless the difference between those points of view is the crux of the fiction, the fiction will suffer from the reiteration. *Haven't I already heard this?* the reader wonders. It's even possible the reader will begin to skip pages. Remember, a fiction's plot should move forward from its inception. Repetition is redundant—and therefore moves the story backward.

DIGRESSION

At the same time, because each character has an individual voice, she'll want to tell us everything about her version of things. The problem is, not every one of those things will be relevant to the fiction you're telling. Yes, well-known writers like John Irving and Tom Wolfe get away with this. But, just like your mother told you, that doesn't make it right.

EGREGIOUS OMISSION

This may be the worst sin of multiple-limited point of view. If everyone knows something happens but you as the author decide to withhold it, you are manipulating not just the fiction but your reader, too. Just as my friend in the example above chose to withhold what her limited point-of-view narrator knew until the end, when everyone but the reader knows something, the reader rightfully will feel manipulated.

If you believe that a multiple-limited point of view is the only way to tell your fiction, I'd challenge you to consider what it would be like if one of the points of view were omitted. What would the remaining point-of-view character *not* know? It's possible that this very item will be just the thing you need to take your fiction to the next level.

Finally, please understand that I personally adore writing multiple-limited point-of-view novels. But because I understand the above limitations, I've tried to use the method in ways that haven't (to my knowledge) been tried before and to create fictions that are surprising and new.

MASTER CLASS

Are there exceptions? Of course. Ian McEwan's *Atonement* and Margaret Atwood's *The Blind Assassin* are primers on multiple-limited point of view. But look at some other contemporary masterworks (all highly recommended, by the way). What's their point of view, and how does the narrator in each of these novels change?

- In Paul Auster's *The Book of Illusions*, college professor David Zimmer learns to love again after his wife and sons are killed in a plane crash.

- In Michael Chabon's *Wonder Boys*, writer Grady Tripp's life develops an antic plot far better than that of the book he can't seem to finish.

- In Mark Haddon's *The Curious Incident of the Dog in the Night-Time*, teenager Christopher John Francis Boone must move beyond a world limited by his autism.

- In Sue Miller's *While I Was Gone*, happily married Jo Becker must repair the damage done when her past returns to upset her contemporary life.

+ In Carol Shields's *Unless*, writer Reta Winters must reexamine her worldview when her insular world is invaded by the demands of the much larger world.

Now, what if each of these were told from the point of view of another character? Auster's book might be told from the point of view of Alma, a character who appears late in the novel. But we'd lose almost everything we know of Zimmer in the process. *Wonder Boys* could be told from any number of points of view because its cast of zanies offers quite a few possibilities. But none of these points of view would be the story of Grady Tripp.

The particular charm and allure of Haddon's book arises from its narrator, whose limited autistic perception is part of the conceit (but a wonderful conceit, in this case) that drives it. If Miller's book were from the point of view of Jo's husband, Daniel, it would be a just another tale of marital discord rather than the nuanced novel it is. Finally, were *Unless* told from any other point of view, we would lose the many digressions that make this Reta Winters's *tour de force*.

OMNISCIENT POINT OF VIEW

So much of contemporary fiction uses limited point of view that an omniscient point of view will often feel "off" to a twenty-first-century reader. The omniscient narrator is sometimes called "the fly on the wall" (though I wonder why a fly would be interested in the goings-on of mere humans) because it is panoramic and sees everything from all points of view.

There's nothing wrong with an omniscient point of view. In fact, it solves many of the problems inherent in a limited or even a multiple-limited point of view. The problems connected with omniscient point of view arise because contemporary writers don't use it properly, instead offering the reader what feels like a limited point-of-view narrator, only to shift to another point of view in the next paragraph, or worse, the next (or even the same!) sentence.

Here's an example: "'You're a big booger,' Linda said, watching with delight as Ted's face turned red. Ted couldn't believe Linda had called him that."

Now, if we deleted Linda "watching with delight" and "Ted couldn't believe," and instead rewrote these two sentences from an omniscient point of view, they would read: "'You're a big booger,' Linda said. To her delight, Ted's face turned red. It was clear he couldn't believe she'd called him that." Do you see the difference? We're now out of the character's heads and with an authoritative external voice instead.

As this example makes clear, there are further problems with an omniscient narrator. There's a sense of removal from what's going on, as if the reader is being told rather than shown. Contemporary readers aren't comfortable with that narrative distance. They don't want to be merely *in* a story, they want to be *lost* in it.

REMINISCENT NARRATOR

The last kind of point of view we'll look at is the reminiscent narrator. You may recall that, in chapter four, I noted that Scout Finch was a reminiscent narrator. A reminiscent narrator has a number of advantages, most especially the wisdom of looking back all these years later.

But there's a caution that goes with using a reminiscent narrator. If the reminiscent narrator isn't necessary to the main narrative, you need to consider why you're using her in the first place. Is it simply because you *are* that narrator? If so, it's possible the story might be better told without that older voice coloring it.

But the opposite is also true. The story told in *To Kill a Mockingbird* requires an older and wiser Scout to not only display its nuances but to utilize Lee's glorious descriptive language. A young girl wouldn't have described those women in that first paragraph (and quoted in chapter four) as teacakes, nor would she have been able to report the events, particularly the trial, as vividly as is done in the novel. A young Scout, in other words, would have been limited by her age in a way the older Scout is not.

In the end, the biggest question about point of view is determining whose story you're trying to tell. The exercise that follows just may help you discover the answer.

MINDING YOUR STORY
Exercise Your Points of View

When writing a story that is based in fact, your initial inclination will be to tell the story from your own point of view, even if you were incidental to the "real" story. So here's a not-so-secret secret: This "real" point of view is usually the least interesting way of telling the story. What to do?

One thing to try is this simple writing exercise: Take a scene you've written from one character's point of view and rewrite it from another character's point of view. This exercise works particularly well with a scene that's based in fact, such as a conversation you had with someone else. When you write the scene from the other character's point of view, that character cannot know what the original narrator is thinking. Nor will that character think the same way. In fact, his thoughts will be very different from the scene's original point-of-view character. Students who have tried this exercise often report that it is a breakthrough one. Try it yourself and see.

chapter 6
GETTING PERSONAL

[1]

When Caroline Meeber boarded the afternoon train for Chicago, her total outfit consisted of a small trunk, a cheap imitation alligator-skin satchel, a small lunch in a paper box, and a yellow leather snap purse, containing her ticket, a scrap of paper with her sister's address in Van Buren Street, and four dollars in money. It was in August, 1889. She was eighteen years of age, bright, timid, and full of illusions of ignorance and youth.

[2]

Lolita, light of my life, fire of my loins. My sin, my soul. Lo-lee-ta: the tip of the tongue taking a trip three steps down the palate to tap, at three, on the teeth. Lo. Lee. Ta.

    She was Lo, plain Lo, in the morning, standing four feet ten in one sock. She was Lola in slacks. She was Dolly at school. She was Dolores on the dotted line. But in my arms she was always Lolita.

The first quotation above is in third person and comes to us from the first paragraph of Theodore Dreiser's *Sister Carrie*. Not only do we get a distinct picture of eighteen-year-old Caroline Meeber as she boards the train for Chicago, we see how little she has not just monetarily but in terms of social skills. The second, first-person quotation is, of course, the opening paragraphs of Vladimir Nabokov's *Lolita*. We don't yet know who's speaking, but boy oh boy, is this a *voice*.

The main difference in these two selections is what we get of these two young ladies. The reader forms a very different picture and has a very different sense of each of them, simply because of the author's choice of person. Dreiser chooses a detached third-person narrator who feels like the author, which offers distance from his character. Nabokov, however, chooses a first-person narrator so aligned with his character's voice as to be indistinguishable. In fact, the author isn't even there.

Person-al Choices

Because narrative voice and narrative distance are so closely intertwined, *how* you choose to tell your fiction is just as important as *what* you have to tell. Your story's person is the equivalent of its way of speaking, and whether you choose first or third (or the less desirable second) person, and whether you choose to align your narrative voice with your character's or take a step (or more) back, can make an enormous difference in not only the story you have to tell but the narrative distance from the story your reader perceives.

Person, for the purposes of fiction, refers to *the person who is telling the story*, what in poetry is called the "speaker." (I like this term because it immediately does away with the incorrect but common assumption that author and narrator are one and the same.) When it comes to telling a fiction, first and third person are your best choices; second person is less desirable, though I'll include it when I go into more depth so you can see for yourself.

Sometimes the easiest way to understand something is to see it, so here's a table that outlines person in fiction:

PERSON	PRONOUNS	ADVANTAGES	DISADVANTAGES
first	I	establishes trust and intimacy; personal, direct, honest	limited point of view, self-indulgent, dishonest?
second	you	subjective, inside character's head	precocious, self-indulgent
third	he, she	perceived distance, potential for insight for both author and reader	detachment, no point of connection for reader

You'll likely notice that the advantage and the disadvantage columns seem to say similar things about each choice. Like so many things about fiction writing, this paradox comes with the territory, so the very directness that comes with using first person ("I was hurt") means a first-person narrator can't know what others are thinking ("She deserved it"). That's because *a first-person narrator is privy to only her own thoughts*. And, while third-person narration offers some distance ("She was hurt, but he felt she deserved it"), it comes with a price: The reader may no longer feel connected to the characters because of that distance.

The easiest way to look at person in fiction is to examine each option on its own merits and demerits, so let's look at first-, second-, and third-person narrations one at a time.

I AM FIRST

A good first-person narrator feels comfortable to both writer and reader, because this is the way we're used to hearing stories told. Further, the

closer the first-person narrative voice is to the character, the more identification there will be for the reader.

Contemporary readers not only take first-person narrators for granted,
they believe what a first-person narrator tells them. That's because there's
an inherent trust to first-person narration. But, in fact, a first-person
narrator is limited by his very subjectivity. Not only can he not know
what others are thinking (though he may guess), he will, as a human
being (or even, I would argue, an alien from a distant galaxy), perceive
things in ways that are colored by his own worldview. Of course, this
subjective capacity to get things wrong is part of the fun of using a first-
person narrator, too.

In fact, because of this subjectivity, a first-person narrator can reveal
more—or less—than what's there. Think about how you color your version of an event in your own favor when you tell your best friend what happened. You can't help it: You want to come out as a hero, not a villain.

In the same way, a first-person narrator will add or subtract according to the story she wishes to tell. At its purest, first-person narration
is unfiltered stream of consciousness, such as the lengthy Molly Bloom
soliloquy in James Joyce's *Ulysses*. But such unfiltered prose is also difficult
to read—and for a reader to connect with.

In summary, a first-person narrator offers intimacy, directness, and
the feeling of honesty. But these very advantages limit what a first-person
narrator can see, know, and say.

ALL ABOUT YOU

Second-person narratives almost always feel precocious. Two relatively
recent examples spring immediately to mind: Jay McInerney's *Bright
Lights, Big City* and Pam Houston's short story "How to Talk to a Hunter."
In both of these narratives, the second-person narrator is really a first-

person narrator being addressed by him- or herself: "You are not the kind of guy who would be at a place like this at this time of the morning," McInerney's novel begins.

Second-person narratives call attention to themselves in the same way that a precocious child demands attention. "See how clever I am?" the second-person narration seems to say, and so it's often difficult to move beyond the device to the work itself. When it works, however, which is the case with McInerney's novel, the reader gets used to the second-person narrator. I don't, however, recommend using second person, especially if you're just starting out.

Still, while I agree with the conventional wisdom that a second-person narrator is not a good idea, I have to add that in early drafts of my novel *Coyote Morning*, Rachel, a seven-year-old narrator, spoke, as seven-year-olds do, in second person. Perhaps not surprisingly, my editor said she felt this device drew attention to itself rather than moving the story along, largely because the other narrations were in third person. I ultimately agreed, albeit reluctantly. Sometimes even now when I read Rachel's sections aloud, I switch them back to second person because it feels truer to the character.

FROM A DISTANCE

Like the opening of *Sister Carrie* at the beginning of this chapter, third-person narration can feel distant, but it doesn't have to be that way. Look at "Wild Horses" in appendix A, and you'll see that it's entirely possible for an author to disappear while using third person.

This example notwithstanding, the main disadvantage of third-person narration is that it can remove an author so far from his narrator that the reader feels as if she's being told the story rather than experiencing it. And because that's the key when it comes to person—how the reader experiences what's she's reading—the decision to use a third-person narrator comes with a second caveat: how distant the narrator will be from the point-of-view character.

Here are two third-person narrations, one using authorial distance and one where the narrator is aligned with the character. The first comes from Henry James's *The Golden Bowl*.

> What befell, however, was that even while she thus waited she felt herself present at a process taking place rather deeper within him than the occasion, on the whole, appeared to require—a process of weighing something in the balance, of considering, deciding, dismissing. He had guessed that she was there with an idea, there in fact by reason of her idea; only this, oddly enough, was what at the last stayed his words.

The second quotation comes from Penelope Lively's *Moon Tiger* and takes place in Egypt during World War II.

> Claudia sits beside the driver. Jim Chambers of Associated News is in the back with a New Zealand correspondent. Conversation has to be shouted above the din of the truck's engine. Claudia feels as though all the bones of her body have been rattled loose and her eyes are red-rimmed and smarting from the dust. The driver, who is protective and amused about this exceptional passenger, warns her to tuck a scarf between her neck and shirt or she will have desert sores like everyone else.

James, it should be noted, hated narrators who were aligned with their authors, noting that the method "put a premium on the loose, the improvised, the cheap, and the easy." But while with Lively's Claudia there is reader identification, with James's Maggie the reader feels removed and distant, *told* what he should think rather than aligned with the character. As I noted earlier, the closer a contemporary reader feels to a character, the more strongly he will identify with the character and her dilemma.

Nonetheless, there are places where narrative detachment is a wonderful thing. Later in the same novel, James crescendos to this:

> And she made a point even, our young woman, of not turning away. Her grip of her shawl had loosened—she had let it fall behind her; but she stood there for anything more and till the weight should be lifted. With which she saw soon enough what more was to come. She saw it in Charlotte's face, and felt it make between them, in the air, a chill that completed the coldness of their conscious perjury. "Will you kiss me on it then?"
>
> She couldn't say yes, but she didn't say no; what availed her still, however, was to measure, in her passivity, how much too far Charlotte had come to retreat. But there was something different also, something for which, while her cheek received the prodigious kiss, she had her oppor-

tunity—the sight of the others, who, having risen from their cards to join the absent members of their party, had reached the open door at the end of the room and stopped short, evidently, in presence of the demonstration that awaited them. Her husband and her father were in front, and Charlotte's embrace of her—which wasn't to be distinguished, for them, either, she felt, from her embrace of Charlotte—took on with their arrival a high publicity.

If James had been aligned with Maggie, the language of this marvelous moment wouldn't be possible. We would lose "the coldness of their conscious perjury," that "prodigious kiss," and that final "high publicity." In a contemporary novel, such language might feel high-handed and false. Then again, why not try?

The Relative Dynamics of Narrative Distance

Narrative distance is a tricky field, but—because perhaps more than any other aspect of fiction writing it affects the way a fiction *feels*—it's important to get it right. One of my students decided she needed some distance from her first-person narrator and tried rewriting some of what she had in third person. The result of this experiment was (for her) delightful and unexpected. Using third person actually brought her *closer* to her narrator, possibly because it gave her the perceived emotional distance she needed to approach the heart of the matter.

Another student was working with shifting first-person narrators, a practice generally frowned upon by editors and agents. Now, shifting first person can work, if each voice is distinct and, far more importantly, if it's the *only* way to tell a fiction. But most of the time, shifting first-person narration is an author's way of discovering her material.

In this student's work, the weakest of the first-person narrators was the one closest to herself. (This is not unusual; we have a hard time nailing ourselves in fiction.) But the strongest was the far more difficult character she had begun the novel to understand and who had initially been a minor character in an entirely different novel. So affecting was this character that I suggested she try writing a novel from his point of view. I've been working with this group a long time and such suggestions don't terrify them as they might students less familiar with my workshops. In fact, in this case, the author, after a brief *Oh no!* moment, became excited and started talking about what she might do with that character. That's when you know you've hit on the right person and narrative distance. There's nothing like the excitement of a fiction taking off.

DON'T SHIFT THAT PERSON!

One of the most common errors I find in early manuscript drafts is shifting person. A piece might begin in third person and then shift suddenly into first. Or, it will begin in first person only to shift to third person in the middle of a paragraph. When I point out these discrepancies to the author, though, he's very often surprised. Why is this?

Sometimes shifting person occurs when writers initially choose third person to write what I call "thinly veiled autobiography," because third person's narrative distance allows them the perspective they need to begin such pieces. Once they get into their narratives, though, some writers get so involved in the writing, they forget they started out in third and start using the "true" first person. While you shouldn't worry about doing this when you're writing a first draft, you will want to make a decision when you go back and begin revising and rewriting. Shifting person in a fiction is a major no-no.

WHAT'S LEFT OUT

When someone tells you a story, you fill in details as you listen. In the process, the story you're being told becomes your story instead. This is what happens when you read, too, which is why, in contemporary fiction, what's left out is just as important as what's on the page. Think about what you're *not* told in *Catch-22*, for example, or about the blanks you fill in any first-person narrative.

Contemporary readers don't want to be spoon-fed everything there is to know; they want to use their own knowledge to draw conclusions. Yes, their picture may ultimately differ from yours, the author's, but if they get a picture at all, you've succeeded. This ability to draw a picture from someone else's words—yes, it's that synecdoche again—is part of the fun of person and narrative distance. Try experimenting with it on your own to see how your fiction changes depending on whether it's first or third (or, if you must, second) person and how closely aligned with your narrator you choose to be. Like the students mentioned above, you may be surprised by what you discover.

MINDING YOUR STORY
A Change of Person

Changes of person have unlocked many a stuck fiction. You may think that the best way to reveal your characters and story is first person, only to stop writing when you get to places that are uncomfortable for you. Or you may feel the distance of third person is necessary but find yourself slipping into first person unconsciously whenever the writing gets rolling.

For this exercise, pick a paragraph from anything you've recently *read*. Determine if it's in first or third person. Then rewrite it, using first person if it's written in third or third person if it's written in first. If you'd like, you can simply use one of the examples in this chapter. Try writing the Theodore Dreiser, Henry James, or Penelope Lively selections in first person, for example, or the opening of *Lolita* in third.

Once you've tried this with someone else's work, do the same thing with a paragraph of your own. In other words, if your paragraph is currently in first person, rewrite it in third; if it's in third person, rewrite it in first. Don't simply go through the paragraph and change every "I" to "he" or "she" (or vice versa). That's cheating! Rather, read the paragraph and then write it without looking at it again, using the other narrative voice, first person for third, or third person for first.

If the paragraph you rewrite seems to work, keep going. Again, don't simply change the nouns and pronouns. Start over. I think you'll be pleasantly surprised by what a change of person can do for a narrative.

chapter 7
LOOK WHO'S TALKING

We ask a lot of our characters. We ask them to be true to themselves (and, though they're less likely to comply, to each other), to reveal themselves through background, gesture, tastes, and surroundings. We expect them to let readers learn about them by the words they use to talk to each other, and we expect them to be as good (or as bad) as those words. But—and here's the rub—as the ones who put words in their mouths, we, the authors, are responsible not only for what they say but how they say it.

Creating believable dialogue isn't as easy as it might seem. Contrary to what you might think, transcribed conversations sound especially flat on the page because real dialogue is full of stops, starts, repetitions, fill words, and idiosyncrasies that have no place in fictional dialogue. Because you, the author, make up the words your characters say and the way they say them, however, you should apply the same diligence to learning how dialogue works in fiction as you would to learning another language, which, in a way, dialogue is.

Speak, Characters

Dialogue is what happens when characters speak out loud. Just as you and I speak (or don't speak) to each other, when characters have things to say, they say them in conversation. But how characters speak is more than mere words. The things they say and the way they say them can reveal a great deal about them, from their ethnic background and class to their relationships with others to whether they're male or female, young or old, married or single, or somewhere in between.

Just like you and me, every character has a different way of speaking. Some speak in fits and starts, some in full paragraphs with punctuation, some slowly, some quickly, some far too much, and some hardly at all. Each of these things reveals something about a character as surely as the clothes she wears and the place she calls home.

MORE THAN JUST THE WORDS THEY SAY

Dialogue's a real heavy lifter: In addition to revealing character (both directly and indirectly), you can (and should) use dialogue to do the following:

ESTABLISH IMMEDIACY

Nothing brings a reader into a scene more quickly than "hearing" characters speak. Here, for example, are a mother and her nine-year-old daughter in Molly Giles's wonderful story "War" (from *Creek Walk and Other Stories*). The mother has just returned from a peace conference in Nicaragua.

> "It's good to be home," I said, not too sure. "But it smells funny. Do you smell anything?"
>
> "Like what?"
>
> "Like socks. Old socks. And ... machine parts? And, I don't know, musk?"
>
> "No. It smells like home to me."

This exchange establishes immediacy by placing the reader in the scene with the characters. But it does many of the other things that I'll discuss in this section, as well.

SHOW RELATIONSHIPS AND ADD TO THE READER'S
KNOWLEDGE ABOUT BOTH CHARACTER AND SITUATION

The relationship between the narrator and her daughter is clear from the exchange above. It's so easy and affectionate, in fact, that we can almost hear each speaking atop the other, as one does in a comfortable conversation with someone familiar. At the same time, the last line lets us know that the mother has either forgotten what home smells like or believes the smell of home has changed, either or both of which reveal a great deal about the situation at this moment in time.

REVEAL THE OPPOSITE OF WHAT
A POINT-OF-VIEW CHARACTER TELLS US

Here's another exchange from the same Molly Giles story:

> She helped me with my bag and we went into the house, talking all the way. "You were in the paper," she said. "They had a big article on the peace conference and they had your name and everything, and Mrs. Bettinger read it to my class and said you were a heroine."
>
> "A what?" I laughed. I was pleased, but I'd seen too many real heroes and heroines in the last few days. "My main job was to make lists," I told Cass. "It wasn't exciting. I gave a few speeches but mostly I just helped people get off one bus and get onto another."

The narrator can't very well tell us she's a hero herself, can she? In fact, it's best that she insist she's not, as this narrator does when she tells us that all she did was make lists and help people get off buses. Nonetheless, the fact that her daughter's teacher calls her a heroine reveals the possibility of it to the reader as well.

GIVE INFORMATION ABOUT CHARACTERS' BACKGROUNDS

Here's still another bit of dialogue from the Molly Giles story. This conversation, in brief flashback, is between the narrator and her ex-husband.

> "Can you stand somewhere else?" he'd said once, when I was trying to tell him about an article I was trying to write. "You're blocking the light."
>
> "That's not *light*," I pointed out. "That's the TV. Don't you know the difference?"
>
> "No," he drawled, dumb, "I don't know the difference. I'm just the bozo who brings home the bacon. You know the difference. Right? So why don't you tell me—like you tell everyone else, over and over, on and on, all the time. Why don't you help me understand the great big world?" he asked. "Why don't you change my life?"

On one level, this story is about how a husband and wife grew apart, and this dialogue reveals a great deal about their background. The story is also about how someone who travels the world promoting peace can't begin to create it in her own home. The best fiction exists on many levels, which is why this story succeeds so beautifully.

Further, though, note how *natural* this exchange, despite its inherent tension, sounds. That "over and over, on and on, all the time," sounds like the way a real person would talk. That's how dialogue should read, as if you can hear the character's voice on the page.

KEEP THE NARRATIVE MOVING FORWARD

Yes, I've said it before and I'm saying it again: Every aspect of fiction should keep the narrative moving forward. This is particularly important for dialogue, as no aspect of fiction can put a reader into a scene—and into a character's mind—more quickly. When dialogue doesn't work, it makes no difference how well a fiction has been moving forward until that point, because bad dialogue will stop it dead. This brings us to some important don'ts.

DIALOGUE NO-NOS

As the examples above show, the best dialogue is so good, the reader barely notices it. The problem is that when dialogue is bad, it not only falls onto the page with a thud, the consequences can be downright laughable.

For that reason, here are some things you *shouldn't* use dialogue for. Dialogue may be a heavy lifter, revealing character, situation, and relationships while continuing to move the narrative forward, but it's not an all-purpose cure-all, though some writers try to make it so.

DON'T USE DIALOGUE TO REPEAT THINGS THE CHARACTERS ALREADY KNOW

"Remember last week when we went to the supermarket and you dropped blueberries all over the floor?"

"Oh, my, yes. The girl who worked at the supermarket whom they called on the intercom to clean them up was pierced in more places than a pincushion. It was all I could do not to stare at her."

I hope that this exchange has "false" written all over it—because it's being used to reveal information to the reader that the *author* wants the reader to know. And not only don't people really talk this way, this information should be imparted using another fictive technique, such as flashback or narrative. Here's how I'd rewrite my example of bad dialogue:

Flashback: The week before when they'd been in the supermarket, Alice had dropped blueberries all over the floor. "Cleanup on aisle ten," they heard over the intercom. "You're in troub—," Myrtle began, stopping when she saw that the young woman who'd answered the call was pierced in more places than a pincushion.

Narrative: The week before when they'd been in the supermarket, Alice had dropped blueberries all over the floor, and a week later, Myrtle was still tsk-tsking about the number of piercings the young woman who'd come to clean up had sported.

DON'T USE DIALOGUE TO REVEAL THOUGHTS A CHARACTER WOULDN'T REVEAL TO ANOTHER CHARACTER

What we (and, by extension, our characters) think and what we say are so far apart that we often wonder if anyone really knows us at all. (As I noted in an earlier chapter, my answer is no, no one does, including ourselves. It's one of the reasons I write fiction, where people *can* know each other, if only fleetingly.) No matter how close your relationship with someone else may be, you'll nonetheless be very careful not to reveal your secret thoughts to him.

So why would you have a character do this? If you're using dialogue to reveal what a character is thinking, you may need to reconsider from whose point of view your fiction is being told. If you're doing it to impart information to the reader, you'll need to reveal it in another way. For example, Alice would never say something like this:

> "Myrtle," Alice said, "I think dropping those blueberries was one more sign of my advancing dementia, which as you know worries me terribly."

But she might *think* this:

> Alice worried that dropping the blueberries could be one more sign of advancing dementia.

Or Myrtle might think *this*:

> Myrtle didn't voice her fears to Alice, of course. There was no sense worrying her.

Or *say* this:

> "Alice, I'm worried about you. You've been dropping things left and right."

In short, don't use dialogue where a simple thought will do the trick.

DON'T, DON'T, DON'T PUT THOUGHTS IN QUOTATION MARKS!

"Where did this idea come from?" No, no! That's improper usage. I may be thinking this (in fact, I am), but because it's a thought, it doesn't belong in quotation marks. Only if I say this to you aloud may I put it in quotation marks.

Instead, I may wonder where this idea came from. Or, if I'm writing a stream-of-consciousness narrative, I may write, Where did this idea come from? I (or she) wondered. I might even use italics to set off the thought, like this: *Where did this idea come from?* I wondered. But put a thought in quotation marks? I'd rather eat crow.

DON'T CLOG DIALOGUE WITH USELESS INFORMATION

This no-no is connected to the instruction that dialogue should keep your narrative moving forward. If a bit of dialogue isn't important, leave it out. This means you can skip "hello." You can skip "how are you." Most of the time, you'll skip names, too, since your characters already know them, and so do your readers.

For an example of what *not* to do, here's a beginning writer's rendition of a telephone conversation.

"Hello?" Mary said.

"Hello? Is Donald there?" the person on the other end of the line said.

"May I ask who's calling?" said Mary.

"This is Ralph."

"Hang on," Mary said. "Let me check." She set the phone down and walked to the bottom of the stairway. "Donald!" she called. "Telephone!"

"I'll get it up here," Donald hollered back down. Mary went back to the phone and waited till she heard him pick up. She didn't hang up, though.

"Hello?" Donald said.

"Donald? This is Ralph. Ralph Jones. I got the stuff. You ready to roll?"

Now I would guess that the only important thing in this lengthy exchange is that Ralph "got the stuff." That, and the fact that Mary doesn't hang up. Here's a more abbreviated and far better way of handling this scene, with the extraneous information in narrative and the unnecessary information eliminated.

The night Ralph Jones called, Mary had answered the phone. She'd meant to hang up as soon as Donald picked up upstairs, but something about Ralph's voice had made her hesitate. That was why she'd heard him tell Donald that he'd gotten the stuff. "You ready to roll?" he'd asked.

BASIC RULES FOR DIALOGUE

Some of this is Grammar 101, but you've got to master the rules in this section for an editor to take you seriously. If these rules are elementary to you, skip them. For everyone else, type them up, print them out, and nail them to your computer monitor.

WHEN A NEW SPEAKER SPEAKS, START A NEW PARAGRAPH

Right: "Did you hear what happened to Mary last week?" Joseph asked.

"No. Do tell!" cried the little drummer boy.

Wrong: "Did you hear what happened to Mary last week?" Joseph asked. "No. Do tell!" cried the little drummer boy.

EVERY CHARACTER SHOULD HAVE A VOICE OF HIS/HER OWN

For a beautiful example of this, return once again to the selections from the Molly Giles story earlier in this chapter.

KEEP DIALOGUE BRIEF

I'm a devotee of nineteenth-century Russian literature, and one of my favorite chapters is the Grand Inquisitor section of Fyodor Dostoevsky's *The Brothers Karamazov*. The success of such a chapter carries with it an assumption that no longer holds true today: One speaker can tell a long story, without interruptions, and his audience will be rapt throughout the telling.

In the age of television, the Internet, e-mail, and even books (remember them?), the art of oral storytelling has gone nearly extinct. Yes, we all still run across the occasional person who can hold a dinner party spellbound with his telling of a story, but there will nonetheless be interruptions, interjections, and asides. In our twenty-first-century world, in fact, no one gets to go on as long as nineteenth-century characters could, so dialogue in which someone speaks without interruption feels awkward and stilted to us.

If it's necessary to your narrative for someone to give a long speech, there are a number of possible solutions.

1. Make it a real speech.
2. Have him write a letter.
3. Break it up with interjections that further the narrative and/or develop character or relationships at the same time.
4. Consider why it's necessary for this information to be imparted this way. If it's important, perhaps it should be done in a scene. (If doing such a scene presents a point-of-view problem, have someone who's there write a letter.)

ALWAYS PUT TERMINAL PUNCTUATION (COMMAS, PERIODS) INSIDE THE QUOTATION MARKS

This one's simple. Note where the comma and period appear in each example and then commit the above to memory.

Right: "I wonder," she said, "if he is going to show up."
Wrong: "I wonder", she said, "if he is going to show up".

Attribution, She Said

Attribution is the way you show who is speaking. Sometimes authors under-attribute, something you can easily recognize: It's that dialogue you read where about three exchanges in you have to count back to figure out who's saying what.

When I come across under-attribution, I know one of two things has happened: Either the author didn't say he said/she said enough, or the characters' ways of speaking weren't varied or distinct enough.

When I write dialogue, I "hear" the attribution as I write. Even in the bad examples above, you'll see that I moved between "said Mary" and "Mary said," and used the attribution to break up the dialogue rather than placing it at the beginning or the end of the spoken words.

Of course, the opposite is also true. It's possible to over-attribute. I would say, however, that if you're good at dialogue, each character's voice will be distinct enough that you can attribute only as necessary—not too much and not too little. For examples of characters who speak distinctly, look again at the examples from Molly Giles's short story earlier in this chapter.

Here are two more rules for attribution:

1. "Said" works best 99.99 percent of the time. (The other .01 percent belongs to "asked" and "answered," but make sure your characters

are actually doing those things.) Having characters equivocate, question, demand, and otherwise quibble slows down your narrative and sometimes makes it inadvertently hilarious. ("I don't know," Mary insisted, or, "Absolutely!" Steve demurred.)

2. Don't use adverbs to "explain" dialogue. (These are called Tom Swifties, as in, "Hurry up," Tom said swiftly.) Let the dialogue and actions do the work. In fact, using action to attribute dialogue serves multiple purposes. Here's Tom again, this time in action: Tom was already at the door. "Come on," he said, pushing it so hard it slammed back against the bricks. "Hurry up."

HONESTY IS THE BEST POLICY

In *On Writing*, Stephen King notes that "Writing good dialogue is art as well as craft," and "The key to writing good dialogue is honesty." As King knows, like all aspects of fiction, dialogue can work for or against you. If, like me, you're a lifelong eavesdropper with an ear for the way people talk (and don't talk) to each other, it can actually be more difficult to create dialogue on the page. If, for example, I included every time my husband said, "Huh?" in response to something I said, I'd have one hundred pages in no time flat. But would my narrative be moving forward? No. Would I reveal something of our relationship? No again, except perhaps that my husband needs his attention flagged *before* I start speaking.

Beginning writers expect a great deal of their dialogue, and some of those expectations are merited. But don't ask your characters to say more than they want for the sake of your story. That part's still up to you.

MINDING YOUR STORY
He Said, She Said

Plays (and films) take dialogue to the nth degree, making it do the work of many elements of fiction that are more difficult to convey in a visual medium. You can use this to your advantage by creating dramatic dialogues that must carry all the weight of a scene.

For this exercise, imagine leaving everything to a director except what your characters will say. It's preferable to try this exercise first in a scene with only two characters and to select a situation with a great deal of conflict already built into it. If you haven't got a scene of your own to try, here are a few possibilities for you to choose from. I've intentionally selected relationship issues because they're easier to practice with.

- a reunion between long-lost lovers
- an argument between business partners over money
- an argument between newlyweds over whether or not to have children
- a reconciliation between an estranged couple

Name your characters and figure out where they are, and then use *what they say* to convey everything that happens in the scene. It may take a few tries, but once you write a successful scene this way, your ability with dialogue will take a giant leap forward.

chapter 8
IT'S NOT WHAT YOU SAY ✦✦✦

Writers who don't love language are like plumbers who don't love … well, perhaps that's not the best analogy. The point is that language is the writer's single most important tool, and understanding how it works, from grammar to the sound of words on the page (because, yes, words that fall on silent pages do make sounds), can help writers move from the merely pedestrian to the magical. After all, what would writing be without words?

The Joy of Words

Language is a writer's most valued and valuable tool. According to Steven Pinker, author of *The Language Instinct*, it's something we pick up as naturally as walking, whether Cantonese or Mandarin if we're Chinese; Tagalog in the Philippines; or English if we're American, British, Canadian, or Australian. So getting language onto paper should be just as simple, right?

Well, it is and it isn't. What separates writing that sounds natural and spontaneous from stilted awkward phrasing is the art behind a writer's fiction, because he's learned *how* to say a thing. The reason good writing sounds as if you're eavesdropping is because the best writers have done the eavesdropping for you, picked the best parts, and then translated them onto the page.

The word *translation* is the key because written language is different from spoken language. If you've ever heard someone read a speech rather than speak from notes or extemporaneously, you know that when something written is read, it sounds awkward and strange. Now, here's the thing: The same holds true if we try to transcribe what's spoken verbatim onto the page. Even the best playwrights, and especially those writing in particular vernaculars like Suzan-Lori Parks, aren't simply taking dictation but using their skills to translate speech into written language. (In the case of plays, of course, these words will get spoken, but it's a heightened speech.)

Many writers (myself included) talk about hearing voices and taking dictation, but when our fictions work, it's because what we've done is translate those voices to the page. So let's take a look at a writer's translation toolbox. While you're likely familiar with most of these tools, you may not have considered them in quite these ways.

THE LADDER OF ABSTRACTION

Linguist S.I. Hayakawa's original Ladder of Abstraction was a political model that illustrated how the more nonspecific the language used is, the more capable it is of obfuscation. Huh? Okay, I cheated: That sentence was written intentionally high on the Ladder, using big words, circuitous constructions, and plenty of dependent clauses; this sentence is somewhere in the middle.

Down here at the bottom of the Ladder, we use direct, concrete language that says, simply and precisely, what we mean to say. In the classroom, I draw a ladder on the board, complete with a stick-figure cow named Elsie at the bottom and her stock-market indicator at the top, and I offer it to you here.

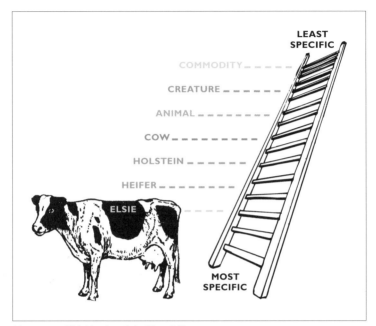

My version of S.I. Hayakawa's Ladder of Abstraction.

At the very bottom of the ladder, we have Elsie, a pretty little Holstein with a name and a personality all her own. On the next rung up, she's simply a heifer, then up again to Holstein, both of which are less specific than Elsie herself but still draw a picture in a reader's head. Next up is cow, less specific still, then animal, then creature, all the way up to the top, when poor Elsie becomes an abstract commodity, traded in futures.

My point with all this is that the most specific words will make the strongest connection with your reader. Governments, of course, seek the opposite course, using the most abstract words to say absolutely nothing, while putting us to sleep at the same time. The more abstract the language, the less accessible the concept, and when it comes to writing fiction, accessibility is everything.

BIG WORD/LITTLE WORD

Did you think you had to know lots of big words to be a successful writer? Well, you do. But that doesn't mean you should use them. I, for one, can get very angry when I come across a word I don't know in a fiction, partly because I already know lots of words and partly because I'm quick-tempered. But worse, here's what happens next: If I decide to look up the word, I put down the book, which, as you already know from earlier chapters, is a big no-no. Remember, the test of a successful novel is whether the reader takes it with her to the bathroom. If she can put it down, you've lost her, and this includes putting it down because she's looking up a word she doesn't know.

But I also find that much of the time a writer uses a big word, he's simply showing off, and I find such displays both obnoxious and annoying. If you want to show off how many words you know, become a lexicographer or a linguist, or write for the government (I'm kidding). When it comes to writing fiction, the key is keeping it simple, creating a work that goes where (and when) your reader goes.

THE THESAURUS SCHOOL OF LANGUAGE

It follows from the above that using a thesaurus to find a bigger, better word is probably not your best choice. Why say "tired," you might think, when you can use "fatigued," or—hey, check this one out!—"lassitude"? Here's my answer to that question, in the form of two sentences. Pick the one that works best for you.

> Tired but determined, Gretchen pushed herself on to the next ridge.

> Beginning to feel overcome by an overwhelming lassitude, Gretchen nonetheless with resolute tenacity propelled herself toward the tantalizing convexity above her.

Yes, I had a lot of fun using my thesaurus to write that second sentence. But if you think it's a better sentence, imagine reading a book full of such sentences. You'd soon be as overcome by lassitude as poor Gretchen surely is by now.

ACCEPTABLE WAYS TO USE YOUR THESAURUS

Word-processing programs' thesauri are so easily accessible that it can be hard to resist their siren call. Do I use mine? Yes, I do, in two specific and very distinct ways:

1. If I find I've used the same noticeable word more than twice within a few pages (or, far worse, in the same paragraph), I'll look for an alternative for one of the uses. But—and here's the important thing—if there's nothing that works as well, I'll leave the word I've used, because using a word whose meaning isn't precisely what I mean is far worse than dual usage.

An example of this is a word like "pass," which in English has not only numerous meanings but is used as different parts of speech, as well. For some of those meanings, no other words will work, but a sentence like "She passed the pass" simply screams for revision. Rather than pull up the thesaurus for this sentence, I'd start from scratch and rewrite it entirely: "Now that the pass was behind her," or "She skirted the pass by taking the low road." The first choice moves the fiction along while the second tells us something about the way she went, as well.

2. As I get older, I sometimes can't find the right word at all. (As someone who's always had a wonderful memory, I prefer to think this problem is the result of an automobile accident a few years ago, though, no, I ain't a kid any more.) I'll know the word I'm trying to remember sounds like "obsess," for example, but means something else entirely. What I do is type in the word I think sounds close—"profess," let's say—using a different color font (or, if I'm writing in a notebook, I'll circle the word). Then I

keep going, because I don't want to let a Missing In Action word slow me down when my writing is going at full heat.

But if the right word doesn't come to me when I read through that new section the next morning (often, thankfully, it does), I'll use the thesaurus to get closer to it. (I used to do this—and sometimes still do—with the alphabetical Roget's I was given so long ago I printed my address and phone number on the inside front cover because I didn't yet know cursive.) Usually, one of the alternate words will be closer, and I'll click on that. Then, I'll click on one still closer. I've found that this scavenger hunt eventually yields the word I'm seeking.

The greatest danger of using your word processing program's thesaurus to find words you can't is picking the wrong word. Results of this are often comical, though they aren't meant to be, so that instead of "She was worried about the weather," we read, "She was apprehensive about the climate." In fact, that one-step climb up the Ladder of Abstraction obfuscates not just what the character is doing but the very feel of the words themselves.

In short, while we're blessed to live in the age of the immediate-gratification thesaurus, you should be careful how you use this tool. A microwave is a similarly wonderful advance, but you wouldn't use it to bake a soufflé. Think of your fiction as a soufflé, and stick with the standard, much slower oven so it will rise just as it should.

TO EUPHEMIZE OR NOT TO EUPHEMIZE

One of my all-time favorite Monty Python sketches is the one about the parrot. You know, the one where the guy walks into the pet shop and says, "I'd like to buy a parrot," and the other guy says, "I have one right here." Then he points to a cage, inside of which is an obviously dead parrot.

"That parrot's dead," says the first guy.

"Oh, no," says the second. "He's just pushing up daisies."

The first guy approaches the parrot, pokes at it a bit through the wire. "He looks dead to me," he says.

"Why, no," the proprietor insists. "He's just resting."

The customer walks around the cage, looking at the parrot. "Dead," he says.

"No, no," says the proprietor. "He's at peace." Et cetera, et cetera.

Of course, translating a Monty Python routine to the page points out the difference between written and spoken language I discussed earlier in this chapter, but you get my point. What the Pythonites are poking fun at here are euphemisms. Euphemisms are words that put a gloss on topics we'd rather not discuss, and in English, that most puritanical of languages, no two topics have more euphemisms at their disposal than death and sex.

Whether someone has passed on, gone to meet his maker, left us, or is still with us in our hearts, he's nonetheless, like that parrot, dead, dead, dead. And whether you're making the two-humped beast, love, or whoopee, it's still sex, sex, sex. Euphemisms may be considered polite elisions in certain circles, but in writing they're just another way of not saying what you mean.

When our father died, many years ago, my brothers and I grew quickly impatient (yes, it's a familial trait) with people who told us he was now at peace or that they were sorry at his passing. "He's dead!" we wanted to holler, probably as much for ourselves as for them. Our father, who hated euphemisms and loved Monty Python, would likely have cheered us on, if he hadn't been pushing up daisies. My advice, pure and simple, is to say what you mean, and call that corpse what it is: dead.

Loving the Language

If there's one requirement of writing that stands above all the others, it's a love of language. I "hear" the words I write on a page, hear their rhythm and the sound they make as they rise and fall. I adore the particular enchantments of English and have also found the difficulties it presents a delight.

My own love of the language is probably why, when a student tells me she doesn't love language, I want to tell her not to quit her day job. She probably shouldn't quit her day job anyway: A few egregious successes notwithstanding, few fiction writers make enough to pay the rent, let alone the mortgage. But the best writers write because they love the language; need to tell stories as much as they need food and shelter; hope to make sense of the world, particularly their own small corner of it; or, simply and absolutely, want to communicate with another human being.

Writers don't write because they want to make millions of dollars. Writing, to paraphrase Ray Bradbury, "is a lonely business," and anyone who doesn't love the language is doomed to fail.

Just as loving a person means wanting to know more about him or her, loving a language means knowing something of its origin. English is a bastard of a language, but it's those very roots that offer it a potential unlike any other.

THE ORIGINS OF ENGLISH

Because of the way first England and later the Americas were colonized, the English language has more roots than bindweed. Never mind how difficult this makes spelling and grammar, which are subjects for the lexicographers and grammarians. What's particularly intriguing about English when you're a writer is its roots in Latinate and Anglo-Saxon languages.

Latinate roots, which include French, Spanish, and Italian, can be found in about forty percent of English words. These are words like "anguish" and "passion," words that are fluid and lofty, and hence feel more abstract. Anglo-Saxon-rooted words comprise about sixty percent of the English language. These words are more everyday, have harsher sounds (such as "shriek" and "crumble"), deal with the concrete, and are hence more direct and informal.

Here, for example, are Latinate- and Anglo-Saxon-rooted words for something we all do in a pinch:

LATINATE	ANGLO-SAXON
odor	smell
perspiration	sweat

Knowing what these linguistic origins can do for writing is marvelous: Depending on the root of a given word, an entirely different effect and mood can be produced. Here are two sentences, the first using Latinate-based words and the second using Anglo-Saxon ones:

> Her manners [from the French, *maniere*] were impeccable [from the Latin, *impeccabilis*].

> Her ways [from the German, *weg*] were blameless [from the Middle English, *blamen*].

Bear with me while we look at these two sets of words. The first, "manners," not only has an effete connotation but sounds more fluid than the Anglo-Saxon "ways." And "ways" not only sounds more everyday, it connotes everyday activities while "manners" does not. In the second set, "impeccable" is a more specialized word than "blameless," which could apply to anything from forgetting to put out the trash to murder. Unlike "blameless," "impeccable" implies something one has learned.

It follows that choosing Latinate or Anglo-Saxon words can affect both scene and character in both obvious and less obvious ways. If, for example, your narrative voice tends to Latinate words but your characters are more working class, it will feel as if the author (you) looks down on her characters. If, on the other hand, your narrative voice is more everyday but your characters flit from salon to dinner party, it will feel as if the author is out of his element.

GOING NATIVE

"Nah, chile, you doan wahn be doon dat," Mammy said. Poor Mammy! Not only is she a stereotype and a cliché, now I've put dialect in her long-suffering mouth. Mark Twain may have gotten away with it, but I would argue that the dialect in *The Adventures of Huckleberry Finn* is one of the book's main difficulties. A far better way to show dialect is in properly spelled words, carefully positioned. Here's *my* Mammy: "Now, child. You don't want be doing that." You can hear her just as well as the first Mammy, can't you? And this time, you weren't slowed down by the colloquial spelling.

The other thing to remember about using dialect is that once in a while is enough. Establish a voice's rhythm and the reader will get it without you reminding her all the time. When I have a character whose first language is not English, her way of speaking English will reflect her first language. Perhaps she will not use contractions. Or it is possible she will use a phrase like "it is possible" in just such a way as I have done in this sentence.

The one exception to this caveat is if you're writing a play or screenplay, where the language ultimately will be spoken rather than read. But written language is meant to be read, and read by someone whose attention is captured and then held. I've said it before and I'm saying it again: Colloquial spelling slows a reader down. Don't do it.

MINDING YOUR STORY
Climb Down That Ladder!

I thought it would be fun to take a piece of government-ese and try to bring it down to the level of the rest of us, but I'm not someone who keeps government documents lying around. My husband, however, is a construction project manager, so I asked him if he could provide a good example. He produced this standard clause in less than ten seconds.

(d) The Contractor agrees to insert terms that conform substantially to the language of this clause, including this paragraph (d) but excluding any reference to the Changes clause of this contract, in all subcontracts under this contract that involve access to classified information.

Here's my translation of that gobbledygook. Note that I don't try to do it word for word.

(d) Both the Contractor and the Owner should use the same terms.

Simplicity. Directness. Clarity. You likely can guess what's coming next. For the paragraph that follows, I bless the Internet, source of all things:

Until the completion of the energy performance analysis at the end of the second year of occupation of the Recorder's Building and implementation of the incentive provisions in the Performance Contract, the County shall have the right to withhold from the final payment an amount up to the Fifty Thousand Dollars ($50,000.00) to secure the obligation of the Contractor to pay the County under provisions in the Performance Contract. In the holding of such funds, the County shall have all the rights, remedies, and obligations that apply to the contract retention held by the County.

Your assignment, should you choose to accept it, is to translate this paragraph into simple English. This paragraph will self-destruct in five seconds. Good luck.

chapter 9
THAT SPECIAL SOMETHING

You've probably heard of authorial voice, about how a strong voice separates good fiction from great fiction. You've probably heard that you need to pay close attention to developing your own authorial voice if you're going to get someone (that editor! that agent!) to pay attention.

Well, here's good news: If you're a human being who knows how to talk, you already have a unique voice of your own. Finding an authorial voice that's equally singular requires both an understanding of the elusive qualities that together create style and a willingness to pay attention to what the masters have to tell—and show—us.

A Style of Your Own

You may know E.B. White as the author of the classics *Charlotte's Web* and *Stuart Little*, but he and William Strunk, Jr., also gave us the finest book ever written about writing in English, *The Elements of Style*. In this stunningly brief manual, Strunk and White spell out everything you'll ever need to know about commas, punctuation, and all other matters of the written word, including White's own hallmarks, brevity, and wit.

"Style," White tells us, is "the sound words make on paper" and is best achieved "by way of plainness, simplicity, orderliness, sincerity." Because we know that a writer like White considered his adjectives carefully, let's look at the ones he uses here. Plainness. Simplicity.

Orderliness. Sincerity. In other words, the best writing achieves its clarity through precision.

Why such an emphasis on clarity? Because there's often the temptation, especially when you're just starting out with this writing thing, to embellish, to use the thesaurus, to use longer words than you might when you speak. As I told you in the previous chapter, it's important that you resist this temptation. Instead, look at how a master does it.

Look, for example, at the first paragraph of Ernest Hemingway's *A Farewell to Arms*, which begins, "In the late summer of that year we lived in a house in a village that looked across the river and plain to the mountains." Joan Didion explored this seminal opening in a November 1998 *New Yorker* article. Here's part of her summary:

> Four deceptively simple sentences, 126 words ... Only one of the words has three syllables. Twenty-two have two. The other 103 have one. Twenty-four of the words are "the," fifteen are "and." There are four commas. The liturgical cadence of the paragraph derives in part from the placement of the commas ... but also from that repetition of "the" and of "and"...

Hemingway's "liturgical cadence" is so familiar to most of us that even if I hadn't told you who wrote that opening sentence, you would recognize Hemingway from his rhythm and word choice. (Didion's style is singular as well. I'd recognize her dependent clauses—"derives in part from the placement of the commas"—anywhere.) You could do worse than spend a month or two practicing Hemingway-esque (or Didion-esque) rhythms. Many writers have done just this, copying Hemingway into their notebooks simply to feel how it is to arrange words as he does. Didion admits that she has. Robert B. Parker, author of the Spenser novels, has done it, as did master short story writer Raymond Carver. I'm guilty, too, as are, I'm sure, thousands of others.

MORE THAN THE SINCEREST FORM OF FLATTERY

But, you object, won't such an exercise turn me into a Hemingway imitator, or worse, destroy my own fledgling voice? No and no. As Anne Lamott says in her classic book about writing, *Bird by Bird*:

> It is natural to take on someone else's style … it's a prop that you use for a while until you have to give it back. And it just might take you to the thing that is not on loan, the thing that is real and true: your own voice.

There's no need to paraphrase Lamott, who's always not only clear but right on the money, no interest required. Lamott is telling us that the most difficult skills—those of craftspeople (and isn't writing a craft?)—are acquired through apprenticeship. In other words, one learns one's trade by chaining oneself to a master.

A marvelous example of this comes by way of an anecdote. My husband, Bob, is a wonderful, self-taught guitar player who learned to play by listening to Eric Clapton. He'd slow the record from $33\frac{1}{3}$ (Remember records? Remember $33\frac{1}{3}$?) to $16\frac{2}{3}$ and play along (and who but a musician would instinctively know that when you cut the speed in half, the key remains the same?).

Bob played along with Clapton until Clapton's licks became second nature. Then he turned the record off and began, as he puts it, "messing around myself." His playing style now, thirty-plus years later, is distinctly his own, but, he insists, owes everything to learning to play with the master first.

This method proves equally powerful to a writer. So if you find yourself imitating the style of the most recent author you've read, rather than berating yourself, just keep on practicing. Remember what Anne Lamott says: You can't master a style of your own without trying on some others first. Sooner or later, your own voice will out.

MINDING YOUR MASTERS

Not only can practicing with the masters help you discover your own style, listening to what they have to say can be instructive, as well. Katherine Anne Porter, for example, whose *Pale Horse, Pale Rider* remains one of the finest short fiction works ever written (and who is one of my own masters), calls style "the writer's own special way of telling a thing that makes it precisely his own and no one else's."

What Porter is saying is that the way *I* tell a story and the way *you* tell a story will be very different. But further, it's in this individual telling that the story will come into its own, because each writer makes a story her own.

A number of years ago, I taught a writing workshop where all the students decided to write (separately) about the character created in the group character exercise. The range of stories that emerged for this one character (who, of course, became a very different character for each student) was remarkable.

Part of this is because each of us has a unique style, so while I'll likely use repetitive phrasing (one of the best things about teaching writing is that you learn to look at your own work more objectively), lots of parenthetical asides (see?), and short declarative sentences to emphasize points, you, having practiced with Hemingway (or your own favorite master), might tell the story in brief, concise, declarative sentences with a great deal lurking beneath their surfaces. But the differences in voice go beyond style. Experience—every last bit of it—colors everything we write. As Eudora Welty notes in *One Writer's Beginnings*:

> *Memory* had become attached to seeing ... and because I recognized in my own continuing longing to keep going, the need I carried inside myself to know—the apprehension, first, and then the passion, to connect myself to it ... I found my own introspective way into becoming a part of it.

Welty's epiphany was the realization that even as fiction writers, it's our selves we put on the page, and our selves that generate our unique voice and style.

WHICH COMES FIRST?

One of the more amusing lessons that arises from reading a lot of writers' thoughts about style is that they don't always agree. Some, for example, note that style arises out of content, while others insist that content doesn't matter. This isn't nearly the paradox it would appear. Here, I'll let a few speak for themselves:

"If there's a choice between style and content, choose content. If you've got the right content, the style comes out of it."

—*Gail Godwin*

"We are not concerned with the ... message ... what matters is [the] song."

—*E.M. Forster*

"You should write, first of all, to please yourself. You shouldn't care a damn about anybody else at all. But writing can't be a way of life; the important part of writing is living. You have to live in such a way that your writing emerges from it."

—*Doris Lessing*

"The writer must be in love with language, with the words themselves, the *sound* of the words on the page, the music they make in meaning."

—*Lynn Freed*

"The writer is always writing, always sounding words, measuring cadences, hearing, feeling, attending to, taking the pulse of, secret rhythms. Content yields to, or crystallizes around, form; form is subordinate to 'voice.' We write by ear, we experiment with 'voice' without knowing what it is."

—*Joyce Carol Oates*

So which comes first, the content or the style? The answer—and it's one to pay attention to, because it has an important lesson about writing as well as about style—is that it depends on the writer, and, like the chicken-and-egg conundrum, isn't worth worrying about, because the answer ultimately depends on you and your own particular way of doing things. The more you write, the more you'll come to trust yourself about such matters.

Taking a Key From Music

You've likely noticed that a number of the writers I've quoted thus far (myself included) use musical metaphors to talk about style. Because I spent some time exploring music theory when I wrote my novel *Dissonance*, this is a language with which I'm especially comfortable.

One of the things I've discovered in my largely autodidactic life is that when you take one discipline's code words and apply them to another discipline, you sometimes get the idea more easily than you otherwise might have. Of course, the term for this is analogy, which science writers use to explain everything from physics to psychics. By its very nature (it's elusive, ephemeral, and a hive of contradiction), fiction writing is a discipline that can be difficult to understand; when, via analogy, you use the language of music theory to look at some of its more obtuse aspects, they suddenly become clear.

A good style, for example, *resonates*, a term that in music theory means increasing a sound's intensity through sympathetic vibration. Now, think about this in terms of an authorial voice that resonates on the page. You feel a connection with that author because of—yes—"sympathetic vibration." It's not something you can easily define without this music metaphor to help. So, here, beginning with style itself, are some other words from music theory that translate style and voice in ways we can apply to writing fiction:

MUSICAL TERM	MEANING
style	the distinctive way a composer or performer uses melody, rhythm, tone color, dynamics, harmony, texture, and form to create a unique sound

melody	the series of tones that form a whole musical idea
rhythm	the speed at which music is performed, the type of note lengths used, and the ways in which notes of varying lengths are grouped
tone color	the property of sound that enables us to distinguish one instrument or voice from another
dynamics	the relative loudness or softness of a sound
harmony	a simultaneous sounding of two or more tones and the way these combinations interrelate
texture	the interweaving of melody and harmony to create a total effect
form	the characteristics that define a specific genre of music

What's particularly fascinating to me about these terms is the way they help us get our minds around not only style and voice, but the way words sound on paper. Whether you're trying to create a mood or work within a specific genre, these terms can help you understand what that specific aspect entails as you move ever closer to your own unique voice.

Being Your Own Translator

Eudora Welty tells us that "Style is a product of highly conscious effort but is not self-conscious," while E.M. Forster calls style "an accent in the novelist's voice." Then there's Stephen King, who reminds us that "the key to good writing … is honesty." While I agree with King, I think writing fiction also requires telling lies to arrive at the Truth (capital T intentional).

No matter how you choose to define it, however, developing a style of your own ultimately involves being your own translator. By this I mean having the ability to translate into words what's heard, felt, or sensed. It's not an easy task. In fact, it's comically (or tragically) difficult, and it brings to mind a conversation I had with my daughter when she was very young. "Can feelings have words?" she asked. I wrote a children's book to attempt to answer that question.

But the real answer is that feelings don't have words, not words that tell us what's happening inside a person. While words like *happy*, *sad*, and *angry* may tell us what a feeling is, that feeling will only be translated for others to feel when a good writer climbs inside a character (or, perhaps, vice versa) and *shows* (there's that word again) how that one individual character feels. That's because the more individual the voice, the more universal the connection.

When I try to explain how fiction does this, I'm forced to use yet another analogy, that of the translation of music onto cassette tapes. (It's likely a similar process is used for CDs, but I'm less familiar with it and so am sticking with what I know.) The recording of music begins with the music itself, sung into a microphone, which uses electricity. When the electronic impulses reach the cassette tape (and you've remembered to press down the "record" button), they are magnetically attached to the tape. Then, when the tape is played back, these magnetic impulses are translated by electricity back into sound, which sounds to a regular listener just like what was originally recorded.

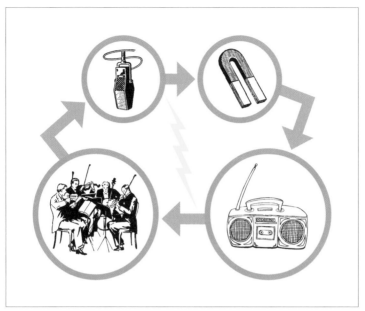

Recorded music is translated through a number of media.

Now, the process of someone reading what you've written is similar. You start with a feeling, a character, a picture in your head. You then translate this picture into words, which you put onto a page. The words (you hope) become a book, which a reader reads. And when that reader reads them, the words are translated into a picture in the reader's head, resulting in a feeling of the reader's own.

Writing that moves us does so because the best stories touch us all, because, again, the universal is most keenly felt in the individual. So, perhaps the best advice about style comes from a pompous old man, advising his college-bound son in one of Shakespeare's best-loved plays, *Hamlet*. "This above all," Polonius tells Laertes. "To thine own self be true."

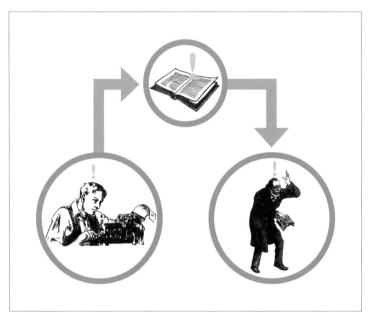

Words are what we use to translate what we're feeling to others.

MAKING MAGIC

There are still days when it seems to me that writing must be magic, that all these things I've learned about it are little more than feints and mirrors. But because I value rewriting as much as writing—because I love to read my first drafts to learn what it is they hope to be—I've learned to pay attention to the ways the magic is made invisible.

In the next two sections of this book, you'll learn how to create your own feints and mirrors. But always remember: Write what you know and the right words will follow. And, as Bob would be first to tell you, practice, practice, practice.

MINDING YOUR STORY
A Voice of Your Own

Open up a book by your favorite author, arbitrarily, to any page, and then get a clean sheet of notebook paper (or, if it's your preference, open a new document in your word processing program, although I think doing this exercise by hand is part of its magic). Now, copy down a paragraph of that author's words. As you do, imagine what it must have been like to write them (and to revise them). Feel the author's rhythm and movement (yes, it's a lot like dancing). For just a moment, *be* Katherine Anne Porter or Ernest Hemingway or Alice Munro.

Next, start a new paragraph, and *without thinking about it*, keep going. You can continue the story you just copied or go off in another direction. What will happen is that you'll move from the master's rhythm and movement into your own. It's *your* voice and *your* rhythm. You just can't help it. Have fun!

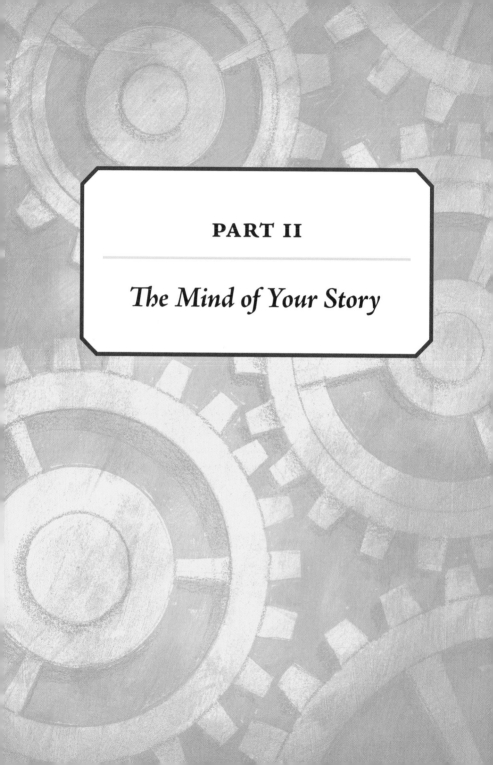

PART II

The Mind of Your Story

chapter 10

THE MIND OF YOUR STORY

Every fiction proceeds at its own pace, a sense of time that the writer creates and the reader senses from the opening sentences. But how does a writer set a pace and control it? How does she slow down, speed up? After all, unlike a racehorse, a fiction's not alert to subtle shifts in its rider. Fortunately, a fiction does have someone else holding the reins—you, its author.

Like a good jockey, you can speed your fiction up or slow it down, all the while maintaining a pace that beats as regularly as your fiction's heart. That's because a fiction's pace is tied to its sense of time, what I like to call the mind of the story.

Time, Time, Time

Like a human mind, a story's mind exists in a present all its own, coexistent with all that came before and all the possibilities yet to come. Don't confuse my use of the word "present" in this context with the grammatical present tense; it's a term I devised to illustrate the movement of time within a fiction.

To envision what I mean by the mind of a story, think about how your own mind operates. Yes, there's this moment now—Oops! It's gone!—but even within this moment, where you sit, perhaps in your favorite chair, reading this chapter, you're thinking about your next appointment or what to make for dinner—both of which occur in a future that's yet to happen—or something your partner said before he or she left this morning or what happened at that meeting yesterday—things that happened in the past. In other words, within each present moment, our wayward minds are everywhere in time.

Now here's the thing: The best fiction operates the same way a mind does (though in a less unedited way than, say, James Joyce's *Ulysses*). This ability to be in many times at once is why I call pacing "the mind of the story." Bear in mind that a story's mind is *not* necessarily the same as the mind of its point-of-view character, although it can be, as in one of the examples later in this chapter. Rather, a story's mind is the progression of its particular moments and all that they contain.

Every fiction has its own present, and within this present, your fiction's mind moves ever forward with each tick of its clock, just like your own mind. At the same time, however, each moment contains other moments—those aforementioned appointments, plans, memories, and regrets—also just as it is in your own mind.

SETTING THE PACE

This said, it follows that the most important aspect of a fiction's pace is establishing the rhythm of the fiction's present. Once that rhythm's been established, when you digress into moments outside the fiction's present in order to richen the brew, that is, when you flash back or imagine the future, you'll nonetheless keep the fiction true to its particular pace. Or, to put it another way, you—and your reader—are always in the mind of the story, no matter where that story goes in terms of time.

For a simple example, let's say your fiction takes place over the course of a three-hour period beginning at 9 A.M. Here's a picture of that three-hour period, which will represent the present of your story.

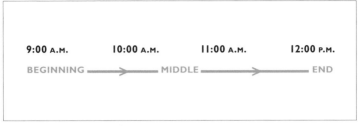

An example of the present of a story.

I've intentionally used an example with a clocklike precision to make my point, but a fiction's present can cover a single moment or a lifetime. The important things are that (1) you choose the best present for the story you want to tell, and (2) once the pacing of your fiction's present is set, you do not deviate from its particular rhythm.

Now, we've all read fictions where, suddenly, the timing feels all wrong. Even otherwise outstanding fiction sometimes slips out of tempo. But like a clock, when pacing works, we don't notice it. In the best fiction, no matter where we are in relation to the story's present, its clock will still be ticking. When a fiction's clock skips, the reader feels it, as surely as if real time had somehow missed a beat. While he can't always articulate what caused the feeling, you, the writer, can now pinpoint its precise origin.

MOVING AROUND IN THE MIND OF A STORY

For an illustration that shows how a fiction's present continues to move forward while its mind moves around in time, let's say your narrator's standing looking out the window, the first cup of coffee of the day in hand. A car drives by. It's a limousine, and he remembers the first time he saw Carol from this very window, as she stepped from the back of a limo not unlike the one that just passed. He remembers how he felt when he first saw her, how he knew he had to know her, and how things were once he did. Then he remembers how it was at the end, when Carol left him here, all alone, looking out the window, just as he is now.

In that paragraph of narrative, I alluded to a number of past events that may actually take pages of scene in flashback to flesh out. For this fiction's pacing to work effectively, as those scenes unfold in the fiction's mind, its clock will continue to tick according to the fiction's particular present. (This isn't a real story. I just made it up. Although, of course, it could be …)

So, if this fiction's present takes place over the course of one morning (that three-hour time frame I suggested above), and now our narrator's cup of coffee has grown cold, we've probably spent one-quarter of our narrative on this flashback. In other words, if the entire present of the fiction is three hours, the amount of time we spend on a lengthy flashback will equal the actual time elapsed according to the fiction's particular pace.

Let's add the above flashback to the illustration of the story's mind I drew earlier:

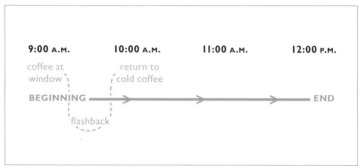

During a flashback, your fiction's clock continues to tick.

Do you see what happened to the story's present while these flashbacks unfolded? It kept moving forward. In the story's present, it's now 10 A.M.

Reading as a Writer

Another way to illustrate how a story's mind works is to diagram a short story to show how its author moves around within that story's mind. Both because I know how it works and because it's included in its entirety in appendix A, I'll use my own story "Wild Horses" for our example here.

While it may not seem readily apparent, the tempo of "Wild Horses" is established in its first paragraph:

> He told her where he was going and he told her when he'd be back. She smiled, and then she asked him, Where are you going?

The mind of the story in this case is also the mind of William ("he," in this first paragraph), even though it is told from a third-person-omniscient point of view. The tempo of the story's present ticks off about a week.

To show how a story's mind works, I like to correlate a fiction's clock to its page count. "Wild Horses" is eight pages long, so I'll begin by marking each page along a line.

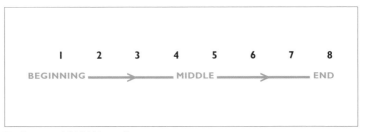

The Present of "Wild Horses."

You'll likely note that I've also marked the beginning, end, and approximate middle of the story in the illustration above. We'll come back to those in a moment. Because this story takes place over a week and is eight pages long, let's say that, in this story's mind, each page is approximately equal to a day as well.

Next, I reread the story and chart its movements in time. When there's a flashback, I mark where it begins and ends on the graph, where the story's present continues to move forward while the story is in flashback. When the drawn line is directly below the story's present, the mind of the story is in that present. When it drops farther below, the mind of the story is in flashback. Lastly, when the drawn line rises far above the line of the story's present, as it does in scenes I and J, the story's mind is either speculating or contemplating the future. The letters refer to scenes in the story, which we've added to the story itself in appendix A; the asterisks represent line breaks.

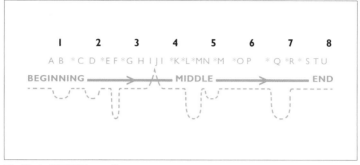

The Mind of "Wild Horses."

Notice in particular how, during the extended flashbacks (scenes L and Q), the story's present—the fiction's mind—continues to move forward even when we're not in it. By the end of the story, it's a week later, but the reader, along with William, has covered all his married years to Althea in these eight pages, via the magic of the story's mind.

An experienced writer will instinctively know where she is in a fiction's present. But even a beginning writer can make sure his pacing is accurate by devising such a graph.

Structuring Your Story's Mind

The example above is a relatively easy one to follow, but there are as many ways to structure a story's mind as there are stories to be told. One of the key things to think about as you consider your story's mind, then, is where your story begins. It's arguably the most important thing in any fiction, not only because it will determine whether your reader keeps reading, but because it forms the initial picture in your reader's head. A good first paragraph will contain the seeds of all that comes after, including whom your fiction is about, what he or she wants, when it's happening, where it takes place, and why the reader should care. But further, as one of my students so aptly put it, "It starts *here* because it's about *this*."

IN THE BEGINNING

"Wild Horses" begins with William coping with Althea's Alzheimer's disease. But why stop with William? Let's consider other examples as well. Why, for example, does "The Metamorphosis" begin, "As Gregor Samsa awoke one morning from uneasy dreams he found himself transformed in his bed into a gigantic insect"? Because that's what this story's about—Gregor Samsa's short unhappy life as a bug. Why does *The Great Gatsby* begin, "In my younger and more vulnerable years my father gave me some advice that I've been turning over in my mind ever since"? Because it's about a young man looking back at the very things in life that that advice addresses.

Even if—*especially* if—you began writing your fiction at a given point, you need to consider whether this is where your fiction really begins. I can't tell you on how many manuscripts I've written, "Begin here," four or ten or even fifty pages from the writer's beginning. Every writer who's seen these words has marveled that she didn't see for herself that this was where the story started. That's because everything else seems to fall into place once you know where a fiction really begins.

I'll address how to determine where your story really begins in more depth in Part III, when I talk about revision and rewriting. For now, you might want to send this idea over to right brain and let it work its magic.

THE HEART OF THE STORY

In a fiction's middle, its heart will be revealed. This may sound reductive, perhaps even obvious, and yet, again, a look at a some examples reveals that the heart of a fiction is nearly always revealed close to the midpoint of the text.

In the case of "Wild Horses," the heart of the story is Althea's love of horses. And where does the reader learn about this? On page 4 (found on page 250 in this book)—the exact middle of the story. Or take another example from a much longer work, such as Carol Shields's last novel, *Unless.* The book has 213 pages, so the heart of the story will likely be revealed somewhere around page 100. Let's see if this holds true. Yes: Here on page 99, I find the following: "Any minute I would lose my balance and then I wouldn't be ... Reta anymore. Like Norah, I wouldn't be anything."

Now without giving away the plot of this remarkable book, it's clear to me immediately that this is the heart of the story, which concerns, among other matters, the choices women make in order to balance family, work, and the larger world. Further, I would argue that Shields's use of the word "balance" in this passage is extremely intentional, the word serving as a fulcrum for everything else. And here that fulcrum poises, right at the center, the book's heart.

THE CONTRACT BETWEEN WRITER AND READER

Lastly, there's a fiction's ending. Take your time here, no matter how anxious you are to type "The End." The best fictions will move more and more quickly for the reader as the end draws near, because the story's mind has become the reader's mind. This is what is meant by getting lost in a book, and once a reader's surrendered, you the writer can do with him or her as you will.

Which is also why a reader can feel cheated at the end of a fiction. A fiction is really a contract between a writer and a reader. The reader offers attention to the writer's tale because the writer offers escape from the reader's own mind. If the contract is breached on the writer's part—if she rushes, is sloppy or redundant, or otherwise compromises the contract with the reader—the reader, rightly, will feel cheated.

"Wild Horses" ends with Althea comforting William, who in many ways is as confused as Althea by what has happened to her. So, in this case, I offer not a happy ending, but one that will resonate for anyone who's ever been confused—in short, all of us.

Paying Attention

Attention to the mind of the story can keep a reader reading even if other aspects of technique are imperfect. For example, I have little patience with what I call "supermarket books" because I find the characters for the most part wooden stereotypes and the writing all too often cliché-ridden and tired. But millions of people, even—horrors!—my friends and family, gobble these books like the potato chips they are. Why? Because these writers know how to lure readers into their stories' minds and keep them there.

Which brings us back to where we began this chapter: A story's mind exists in a present all its own. The key phrase here is "all its own." If you consider the worlds of Harry Potter's Hogwarts or Frodo Baggins's Middle Earth, of Edward P. Jones's Virginia or Washington DC or Harper Lee's Maycomb, you are immediately back not only in a setting but in a *world* not your own, to which you happily surrender.

Creating a similar world in your own fiction means creating a tempo and structure—your story's ever-ticking present—that are familiar enough to the reader that she'll slip off her shoes and stay awhile. Yet you must also create a movement between present and past and future—the story's mind—unfamiliar enough to keep her guessing, and so, reading on. In short, offer your reader a story with a mind of its own and she'll be happy to stick around. Wouldn't you?

MINDING YOUR STORY
The Mind of Your Story

Now that you see how pacing works, you can try working with it yourself. Pick a scene where you feel some backstory is needed. Now give your character a cup of coffee and a trigger like that limo noted early in this chapter. See what memories the trigger unleashes for your character. See how long the memories take. When you get back to your story's present, time should have moved that much farther along.

To check your pacing, draw a chart like those in this chapter, using the length of time your fiction covers as your story's mind. Then draw a line that represents the flashback and see where you return to the present of the story.

If the flashback you created is too long, consider picking up the fiction's present later in the story's mind. If it's not long enough, jump back in and see what else it has to tell you. You can't hope a reader won't notice when pacing is off. You have to fix it so it works. Understanding how a story's mind works will help you make it so.

chapter 11
MANAGING TIME

What do *chronos*, Greek for "clock time," and *kairos*, Greek for "holy time," have to do with the mind of a story? Everything. One starts your fiction's pace and keeps it ticking, while the other uncovers your fiction's heart. In chapter ten, you learned how to establish pace by creating a fiction's particular rhythm. The next step is to maintain that rhythm throughout the fiction while at the same time moving the plot forward so your reader keeps reading and reading and reading.

Chronos *and* Kairos

In *chronos*, each second, minute, and hour has a value equal to every other second, minute, and hour. Put another way, *chronos* refers to constant, unchanging time, scientifically measured and always the same.

But remember that last minute before the bell rang in grade school, when you watched the clock tick off each second? Time seemed to drag, didn't it? Or remember, conversely, how time just flew by when you were hiking in the Grand Canyon—or painting it? By the very language we use when we talk about such moments—"time dragged" or "time flew"—it seems that *chronos*, with its unvarying precision, doesn't apply. In fact, it doesn't: Each of these instances is an example of *kairos*, which refers to the emotional experience of time, the way we—and by extension, our characters—*feel* about a moment.

The trick to managing time within a fiction is to employ both *chronos* and *kairos* to their best effects. Your fiction's clock, which you set in motion when you establish the mind of your story, will continue to tick like a metronome in *chronos*. But the *emotion* of your fiction will happen in *kairos*, holy time. This means that the moments that matter most to your fiction will be the longest and most vivid. But when they're over, your fiction's clock—its *chronos*—will have ticked that much farther along.

KEEP THE CLOCK TICKING

Once you grasp how *chronos* and *kairos* work in a fiction, you can't imagine why you never thought about them before. But because it's not always easy to make the mental leap to understanding these concepts, examples are particularly important.

Let's say, for example, that your fiction takes place over the course of one day. Your hero, Joe, gets up in the morning, and you spend the first paragraph on his getting up and getting going. This establishes the *chronos* of your story; in this case, one paragraph equals one hour.

Now, not every paragraph will show another hour. Whenever you are articulating a moment that's at your fiction's emotional heart, you'll likely need many paragraphs to show a few moments in time. But—and here's the key—when those moments are over, your fiction's *chronos* will have moved along by X number of ticks. So if you spent, say, four paragraphs in *kairos* on a pivotal scene in a fiction with the one-paragraph-equals-one-hour example above, the fiction's *chronos* will have moved four hours ahead, no matter how long the scene itself really took.

The drawing on the next page shows how this works. So you can see how a different *chronos* might work, I'll make the *chronos* here one page equals two hours. The bar represents a scene that takes three pages. So, when the scene is over, the fiction's *chronos* is six hours farther along.

	top of page 1	top of page 2	top of page 3	bottom of page 3
CHRONOS				
KAIROS	8:00 A.M.	10:00 A.M.	12:00 P.M.	2:00 P.M.

In this story's *chronos*, 1 page = 2 hours. The three-page scene covers only a moment, but the fiction's *chronos* ticks six hours farther as it does.

APPLYING *CHRONOS* AND *KAIROS* TO A FICTION

Whenever I introduce *chronos* and *kairos* in a class, I'll practically hear the clicking of minds as students all over the room get it. Students then bombard me with examples of fictions they suddenly realize make use of this concept (though I must add that there's a good chance most fiction writers haven't thought it through to this extent).

Can you think of a fiction you recently read that illustrates how *chronos* and *kairos* work? Applying this idea on your own is a great way to make it click. Consider first the fiction's *chronos*: How much time elapses from the beginning to the end of the fiction? Next, note its page count. When you've established these two givens, divide the time elapsed by the number of pages to arrive at its *chronos* and see how its mind progresses. Finally, examine the fiction scene by scene. You may find it helpful to draw a diagram like the example above to help you see the fiction's *chronos* and *kairos* in action.

Going Back in Time

If your fiction's *kairos* occurs in the past, its flashbacks will unfold with its *chronos* ticking away. As in the previous chapter, I like to use a cup of coffee to illustrate how this works:

> Joe took a cup down from the cupboard and poured himself some coffee, then sat down at the table. It was the cup Mary had given him on their trip to Morocco, the last trip before their breakup. They'd discovered the little stall set apart from the others ...

You'll continue on with this pivotal scene (that will, say, illustrate how differently Joe and Mary view the world) to its conclusion, and then you'll return to Joe and his coffee, which in the story's *chronos* has now grown cold. The cold coffee lets the reader know that while the scene has occurred in *kairos*, the *chronos* has continued to tick.

MASTER CLASS

When I thought about how many times I've given this example, I realized how many future fictions might have cooling cups of coffee unless I encouraged all of you to tick off your *chronos* in some other way. So here's another possibility: Penelope Lively's Booker Prize–winning novel *Moon Tiger* provides a more intriguing and possibly more effective way to keep the reader in your story's mind, no matter where you are in time.

Moon Tiger's "present" unfolds as Claudia lies on her deathbed. "I'm writing a history of the world," she tells a nurse in the novel's first paragraph. This establishes the book's *chronos* as the few days it will take her to die. At 208 pages, that rounds to about one hour every three pages, or twenty minutes per page. (I have come up with this based on an observation made by a character on page 181: "That was two days ago. You're a bit muddled up." "What have I been doing for two days, I wonder?" Claudia asks.) The *chronos* of *Moon Tiger* moves in and out of the story's—and in this case, Claudia's—mind as the *kairos* unfolds in scene.

One scene, for example, unfolds from page 82 to page 87. Even though we don't return to the novel's present (Claudia in her hospital bed) before moving on to the next scene, we nonetheless know from the calculations above that the novel's mind is five to six hours farther along at the scene's conclusion.

LINGUISTIC TRIGGERS

Like most deathbed novels (if not a genre, it should be), *Moon Tiger* spends the majority of its time in its protagonist's past. Lively uses what I call linguistic triggers to move between her novel's *chronos* and *kairos*. Linguistic triggers echo between a fiction's present and flashback, helping the reader keep her place, as in this example early in the novel. Claudia, in her mind (which in this case is also the story's mind), considers her father and "the rocks from which we spring and to which we're chained ..." Lively then leaps (via line break) back to the novel's present tense, where we find this:

> "Chained to a rock," she says. "What's he called?"
>
> And the doctor pauses, his face a foot from hers ...

The linguistic trigger here is "rock."

After few more pages, we find movement between two different time periods in Claudia's past. Because Lively has already established that linguistic triggers will move us between the novel's *chronos* and *kairos*, this leap is not at all difficult for the reader:

> My Lisa was a dull child, but even so she came up with things that pleased and startled me. "Are there dragons?" she asked ...

***

There is a dragon on a Chinese dish in the Ashmolean Museum ...

The linguistic trigger here, of course, is "dragon."

Whether you signal movement in time via your own version of that cup of coffee or linguistic triggers, the main thing is to be consistent.

SCENE AND NARRATIVE

Quite simply, a fiction's drama will occur in scene. What matters to your fiction will—no, *must*—be shown vividly. What doesn't matter—getting from one place to another or from one time to another—will be told in narrative. If, for example, you need to get Joe from Albuquerque to Dallas that morning, but nothing of importance to the story happens during the trip, you'll use narrative: "Once Joe was off the plane in Dallas ..." or "It wasn't till he was on the elevator in Dallas that Joe ..."

Of course, you *could* use that air time for some *kairos* to reveal backstory, such as "Joe hadn't flown since he and Mary got back from Morocco ...." After all, your fiction's *chronos* is ticking. But if you do choose to have a flashback, it must be relevant to that particular moment in the fiction. (I'll discuss this concept in more depth in the next chapter.)

It's important to remember that the rules of plot trajectory apply to every scene, as well. This means that every scene will have a purpose. Every scene will offer forward movement. A change will occur. Things will be different at a scene's end than they were at its beginning. A question will be answered. The reader will know something that he didn't know at the scene's beginning.

If nothing changes from the beginning of a scene to its end, either the scene is not important to the larger fiction or you have not yet uncovered its importance, and, no matter how much you love it, it may end up on the cutting room floor (which we'll discuss in great detail in Part III of this book).

Your Hardworking First Paragraph

A fiction's first paragraph will establish its *chronos*, setting the pace for the rest of the book. At the same time, it should also establish suspense, introduce your protagonist, set up the situation, and reveal the setting.

That's a lot of work for a first paragraph, but when it works, the reader won't realize how much you're doing. Here, for example, is the first paragraph of my novel *Coyote Morning*:

> On that Monday morning in April, Alison Lomez watched through her
> kitchen window as her seven-year-old daughter Rachel shuffled to the end
> of their gravel driveway, where the school bus would stop for her. At first,

Alison thought it was a dog that trotted up and sat down next to Rachel, a small yellow dog that reached to Rachel's chest. Dog and girl watched the empty road that wound down from the mesa. Whose dog? Alison thought, and then, what kind? And then, coyote. At this, the animal slowly turned its head, and looked Alison squarely in the eye. As Alison watched, Rachel bent to say something to the animal before resuming her vigil.

Now, here are the facts and figures you need to calculate *Coyote Morning's chronos*: *Coyote Morning's* "present tense" covers three days, or seventy-two hours. The novel is 196 pages long. So, every page equals approximately twenty minutes.

This paragraph, however, covers just one moment in time. This, in fact, is how I will present each of Alison's scenes, with time seemingly elongated, as it is here. In this paragraph, it's as if Alison's adrenaline has kicked in, slowing the moment, increasing the horror.

Now, *Coyote Morning* has a second protagonist as well. She's a far more internal character than Alison, so in a way I must establish a separate *chronos* for her, which is nonetheless true to the novel's primary *chronos* (Alison's). Here are that character's first three paragraphs:

Where Natalie Harold came from, the wildest thing she ever saw was the motion of an invisible bird in a tree. Everything was close there, close and grey, and so when she first saw the sky over the desert she knew it was the place she'd never even known to dream, and she knew she was home.

When Natalie was the first person to walk the ditch bank in the morning, as she was today, the S's of night lizards would draw her paths for her. Small catches of coyote fur might dandle from chamisa; small patches of rabbit fur below suggested a recent repast. This early, the sun had not yet crested Sandia Mountain to the east, the mountain that the Indians called Turtle Mountain not only because of its shape but also because of its seeming motion, and some mornings, the air might still tang from a late evening rain, the sand still clot with the last of its moisture.

As always, Natalie walked slowly and, like most Valle Bosqueleños, she carried a big stick. The stick was to ward off loose dogs. She walked slowly in case today was the day she would finally see a coyote, her long-held and most cherished dream.

Note that, like Alison's opening section, Natalie's also covers only a moment in time. But the pace in this section is slower than in Alison's, the words and sentences longer. Along with Natalie, the reader sees more details, visualizing the place as eternally separate from the moment, even while Natalie (and the reader) is in it.

As if I hadn't set myself a difficult enough task, there are other voices in *Coyote Morning*. Each chapter opens with a "Coyote Fact" that establishes the chapter's focus in some way. Then, there are letters to the editor of the small village's biweekly paper, which act as a sort of Greek chorus and, while they can fit within the novel's *chronos*, really exist outside it. There are also occasional "Coyote Logs," courtesy of the village's Animal Control Division. And finally, there's a third voice, Alison's seven-year-old daughter Rachel, whom you met briefly above. Her sections end each chapter. Here's the end of chapter one:

> Did you get a *dog?* says Suzy Charles. Rachel doesn't know what she means when she says that, so she asks her, What do you mean? Suzy says, I saw you waiting for the school bus with your dog, so then Rachel says, That wasn't a dog that was *my coyote*, and then she laughs because she *wants* it to be her coyote. Suzy Charles laughs too and Rachel decides she can be her friend today. His name is Chris, Rachel says. No, Suzy says, that's your *daddy's* name, and Rachel decides she's not her friend today anymore and maybe not tomorrow, either.

Now, without me telling you, what do you notice about the length of time this paragraph covers? That's right: Just like Alison's and Natalie's sections, it takes place over only a moment. In other words, all three of *Coyote Morning's* voices use *kairos* in the same way. Intentional? You bet. I'm a *very* intentional writer.

Once you understand how *chronos* and *kairos* work, you can begin to make imaginative leaps just as I do in *Coyote Morning*. In fact, the exercise below will show you that you likely already have.

MINDING YOUR STORY
Manage Your Time

There's a good chance you have instances of *chronos* and *kairos* in something you're working on but simply haven't thought of it in this way before.

For this exercise, choose a fiction of your own for which you've completed, at the least, a first draft. Now, establish the following:

1. *The fiction's* chronos: How much time does the fiction cover from beginning to end?
2. *The fiction's length*: How many pages long is the fiction?
3. *Time elapsed per page*: Divide the time (#1) by the number of pages (#2).

Next, pick a scene that's pivotal to the fiction. (Actually, every scene should be pivotal, but because this is a first draft, there may one scene that's particularly vivid or strong.) Answer these questions about the scene:

a. How many pages does this scene take?

b. How far has the fiction's *chronos* ticked during this scene?

c. Does your story's mind resume X number of pages farther along in its *chronos*?

Finally, consider the scene itself. How much time elapses *in the scene*? Is this a pattern that you follow throughout the fiction, or do some scenes cover moments while others cover years?

If your fiction has been feeling "off" and you haven't been able to figure out why, answering these three sets of questions may provide the key. If you've handled pacing well, they will nonetheless provide you with a formula against which to check any changes you make to ensure the rest of your fiction maintains the same *chronos*. Either way, these questions can help you determine what sort of *chronos* your fiction should have.

chapter 12
KEEPING THE PACE

Maintaining a fiction's particular rhythm while still moving the plot forward can seem to require managerial skills equal, if not superior, to the best of MBAs. But once you grasp the concepts of the mind of your story and *chronos* and *kairos*, you're ready to explore ways to move things along or slow them down. In this chapter, you'll learn how everything from word choice to sentence length can affect a fiction's rhythm, as well as how the ordering of moments in your fiction, from the perfect beginning to a climactic moment, can affect your reader.

Hurry Up and Wait

Kairos is as much about how a reader experiences a fiction as it is a reflection of your characters' emotional moments, and word length, sentence length, and paragraph length contribute to (or detract from) that experience. But which choices affect the way a passage feels may surprise you.

Let's start with two paragraphs about the same moment in time. Which moves faster? Why?

I. Joe bounded to the car. Fiddling with the gearshift, he finally found reverse. Roaring out of the garage, the tires squealed as he quickly shifted into drive. He sped out of the cul de sac. When he got to the highway, weaving in and out of traffic as fast as he could, he recalled the telephone conversation he'd just had with Mary ....

2. Joe hopped into the car, jammed it into reverse and roared out of the garage, then squealed out of the cul de sac to the highway, narrowly avoiding a Mustang that changed lanes as he turned. *I want a divorce*, he heard Mary say again just as a horn sounded behind him. He flashed the driver a finger then cut back into the other lane again. Another horn blared.

I tried, with some difficulty, to make every mistake I could in the first paragraph. (This was very difficult for me, and I learned something here: Don't write the bad paragraph first. It makes writing the good paragraph harder.) I used action words, shorter sentences, lots of movement, and a flashback to what precipitated Joe's anger.

All of this is what I should be doing, right? Yes, but (of course there's that "but") instead of using active verbs, I chose participles (-ing constructions), which slow down the narrative. I tried to keep my sentences short, but instead of speeding the action, the short sentences, with their choppy one-syllable words, slow it down. Finally, suddenly, in the midst of the action, I leap out of it, leaving the reader between lanes and in a flashback, dangling.

In the second paragraph, I moved as fast as Joe. The verbs are active, and the action moves quickly as a result. I didn't have time for a lot of periods and sentence breaks because Joe didn't either. Joe's mind is racing in *kairos,* and so is my paragraph: zoom, zoom, zoom. Even Mary's words cut in and out: Rather than "recalling," Joe "hears" Mary's words. See—no, *feel*—the difference?

SLOWING DOWN

The same rules apply when we want to slow down the pace. You've probably learned you should use longer words and longer sentences to slow the pace, but that's not necessarily true. I'll illustrate by using a second set of examples. The good example comes from Carol Shields's *Unless*. The bad rewrite is all mine. Can you tell which is which?

> 1. I watched her roll the scarf back into the fragile paper. She took her time, tucking in the edges with her fingertips. Then she slipped the parcel into her plastic bag, tears spilling freely now, wetting the pink kernel of her face. "Thank you, darling Reta, thank you. You don't know what you've given me today."

> 2. As I watched, she proceeded, ever so slowly, to fold the paper, inch by inch, around the scarf, taking her time and using her fingertips to tuck in the edges before finally slipping the box into her plastic bag, at which point she was crying so hard, her face was wet as she thanked me through her tears.

I again had a hard time writing the bad paragraph. It's the second one. My rephrasings are vague, participial, and circuitous, and so do nothing to help the reader experience Reta's *kairos*. Instead, it's so convoluted that the reader has trouble staying in the mind of the story, period.

In fact, in each of the two bad examples above, the reader is repeatedly pulled out of the character's experience. To keep your reader in the mind of your story, the language you use must reflect your character's *kairos*. So, the closer the mind of a story is to the character's *kairos*, the more effective your pacing will be.

Ordering Your Story's Mind

Everything that happens in your fiction should occur at the moment when it will evoke the greatest response from a reader. This means that even if your fiction's time frame begins here at point A and then moves forward till it ends at point B, the mind of your story doesn't need to progress lineally.

Instead, the mind of your story should move forward *emotionally*, building momentum toward its climax. Yes, scene A may have occurred in time before scene B, but your fiction may achieve far more emotional impact if scene A occurs *after* scene B. In other words, the placement of each scene must be relevant to its emotional impact in the mind of your story.

Consider any story by Alice Munro and you will see what I mean. Munro begins almost all of her stories in a particular moment that takes place long before or after its primary time frame. She then moves back and forth in her story's mind until she arrives at another particular moment, also often long before or after the story's primary time frame.

In "Runaway," for example, Munro begins with one of the characters, Carla, seeing Sylvia's car drive past as she arrives home from Greece. This moment initiates the story's present action, but we are soon (on the next page) in the backstory of how Carla and her husband, Clark, have come to be in this place at that time. On the page following, we move further back the same summer, to the facts of Clark's temper and, more specifically and importantly, to the disappearance of Carla's little goat, Flora.

Next, Munro moves briefly to Carla's life before Clark and her family's disdain for the lifestyle she's now chosen (though she hasn't corresponded with them—this is conjecture on the character's part), before we are back in the story's present with Carla once more considering the way Clark picks fights with others, and then, to Flora's disappearance. There is then a brief exchange between Carla and Clark ("She phoned," he tells her, relieving her of the worry of having to tell him Sylvia's back.

After a page or so of backstory on how Carla and Clark met, Munro introduces Sylvia's late husband with a few telling details about him, including the fact that Carla has told Clark he made a pass at her—even though he didn't. "And in one part of her mind it was true," Munro writes, just before she shifts into Sylvia's POV, about ¼ of the way into the story.

Sylvia has a romanticized image of Carla that is at odds with what the reader has already learned about her, and she's not only looking forward to seeing her, she's spent some time in Greece selecting several gifts for her. After a lengthy scene between the two women, Sylvia mentions Flora. "'She's gone,'" Carla tells her, before bursting into tears.

"With every moment…the girl made herself more ordinary," Munro writes, and then, in a paragraph of its own, "It turned out to be the husband." Despite—or perhaps because of—this, Sylvia comes up with a plan to help Carla get away from Clark.

From this halfway point through the next four pages, we are in the present of the story as Sylvia brings this plan to fruition. Then, with Carla finally on the bus on her way to Toronto, Munro shifts to the backstory of Carla and Clark as it was told to Sylvia while they got Carla ready—a far different story than the one we've read earlier—up until the moment Carla ran away with Clark.

Back in the story's present, Sylvia begins to second-guess herself. She's interrupted by a knock on the door, at which point the narrative shifts back to Carla, on the bus. Carla is already reconsidering, beginning with the idea that her running away was all Sylvia's idea and doing. By the time the bus arrives at the next stop (two pages later), Carla gets off the bus and calls Clark.

The knock on the door is Clark, of course (so you see how Munro has moved forward in time, as well as backwards), after he's brought Carla home again. After a confrontation between Sylvia and Clark, Flora (the missing goat) appears to Sylvia magically, and her appearance dispels the tension.

Munro shifts to Carla's point of view for the final three pages. Here we learn that, a month or so later, things are good on the surface, but that Carla has been ignoring a gathering of buzzards far off in a field. We also learn that Sylvia has written Carla a letter about Flora's miraculous reappearance. Carla burns this letter.

But she can't let go of the thought that one day she will go down to the place where the buzzards were (see how time has passed, with this verb?) "She might find bones," Munro writes. But she doesn't go.

From the story's present of one summer, Munro has moved effortlessly back and forth in time, heightening the emotional effect of this story in such a way that it is nearly unbearable. You may argue that you'll never write like Alice Munro, and you may be right, but that doesn't mean you can't study how Munro orders her stories' minds to achieve the greatest emotional effect. In addition to "Runaway," I recommend "Friend of My Youth," though almost any Munro story is a marvelous instructor of fictive technique, and of pacing, in particular.

THE RIGHT BEGINNING FOR THIS FICTION

As I discussed in the last chapter, your first paragraph establishes your *chronos*, setting the pace for the rest of your fiction. But that hardworking first paragraph is doing still more than all we've already attributed to it thus far: It's also the *only* moment at which this particular fiction can begin.

My story "Wild Horses," which we've looked at a number of times already, can once again serve as our example here. This story begins with William trying to deal with Althea as she is now, from whence the mind of the story moves all over William and Althea's life together just as William's mind might. If the story were instead told in a linear fashion, beginning with, say, the moment Althea first discovers the wild horses, or still farther back, when they were first married, the emotional impact of the story would be not just depleted but nonexistent.

AND, IN THE END ...

The climactic moment of a fiction affects not only that moment but every moment that came before it and all that will come after. Like a stone dropped into a pond, it ripples outward. Nothing is the same once the climax has occurred. It's the largest *kairos* in a fiction. Rather than cover the same territory twice, though, I'll show you one example of how this works at the end of this chapter, when we look at the ending of "Wild Horses" in another context.

THE RELEVANT TIME SHIFT

Remember that your main goal is to keep your fiction's mind moving ever forward. Sometimes, however, the best *kairos* occurs in a character's—and the fiction's—past or future. It's at these moments that we go back or forward in time, either via a flashback or a time shift. The key is to ensure each time shift occurs at the right moment in your fiction.

A character's past and future are always relevant to her present. Not only are we products of everything that has gone before in our lives, but our hopes and dreams for the future affect what we do now as well. And just as certain parts of our own lives are more relevant at one moment than another, the moments of our characters' pasts and futures must be relevant to the moments in which we reveal them. In other words, the time shift you choose to reveal must color your fiction in some important way at the moment you reveal it.

This means a number of questions will come into play whenever you think it's appropriate to move around in time. Let's look at each of them.

1. WHEN IS A TIME SHIFT APPROPRIATE?

As any agent or editor will tell you, it's best to get your story's present going at a good pace before you slip into its past so your readers become emotionally invested in your protagonist and feel thoroughly grounded in time and place before moving them off somewhere else. One of the errors I often see in early drafts of novels is a time shift in the first five pages. A good rule of thumb is to get at least a tenth of the way into your narrative before you begin going back in time. In a 75,000-word novel, this would translate to 7,500 words, well into your story's present narrative.

This said, time shifts can occur anywhere throughout a fiction. Just don't drop into flashback arbitrarily because there doesn't seem anything better to do at the moment. This leads to the next question.

2. WHY THIS TIME SHIFT NOW?

You can't shift time simply because there doesn't seem to be anything going on in your fiction's present. As I said above, the past you choose to reveal must color your fiction in some important way, but more than this, it must color your fiction *at this moment in its telling* in some important way. This particular flashback must matter *now*, at this particular moment.

I had a great deal of fun moving back and forth in time in my short story "Men on White Horses" (yes, there are a lot of horses in my short fiction). In the passage that follows, for example, I move from a photographic display on the protagonist's refrigerator directly back in time to her childhood:

The front of the nonworking refrigerator serves as impromptu photo display. Here are Franny's grown daughters, Leslie and Marie, and here's her sister Frieda, pretending she's about to fly off the Whirlpool Trail. They could hike that trail in their sleep, and in her dreams Franny still does, the sheer drop down to the swirling water below never signifying danger as it ought to but instead something familiar and true.

Their father told them that when he'd been a boy, he sometimes found arrowheads along the trail. Animals—deer and wolves, he said—had made the trail down to the river, and then the Indians, stalking the animals, widened it with their stealthy footsteps. Now, us, he said. We're followers, not pathmakers. Listen. Pay attention. Sooner or later, you'll find an arrowhead of your own.

Franny strained to pay attention. She reminded herself to pay attention. And yet when something unexpected happened it always surprised her. Like that time Frieda had suddenly shoved her against the sheer wall along the trail ...

Look at how many different moments from Franny's past occur in these two-and-a-half paragraphs. There's the story's present (in present tense, in this case). There are Franny and her sister Frieda, hiking the Whirlpool Trail as girls. There are things their father said to them, then two sentences in the narrative present (in past tense) before a shift back to a specific moment when Franny and Frieda were hiking the trail. For Franny, at this moment in her life still surprised by the unexpected and still seeking her own "arrowhead," each of these past moments colors her present in a significant way. And for the story, each moment heightens the *kairos* precisely as I want it to.

3. IS THIS TIME SHIFT FOR ME OR FOR MY READER?

When we know as much as we do about our characters, it's tempting to try to squeeze it all into the fiction. But many of the things we know simply *don't matter to the fiction we're telling.* No matter how interesting an episode from a character's past may be, if it doesn't color the current story in some important way, it's likely there for you rather than for your reader.

4. DOES THE STORY NEED THIS PARTICULAR TIME SHIFT?

This same rule holds true for time shifts that do nothing to move your narrative forward. Extraneous information is extraneous, whether it occurs in the past or present of a fiction. Remember, the most important purpose of a time shift is to keep your fiction moving along while revealing something from your character's past that colors his present in some significant way. You've got to be utterly ruthless about weeding out unnecessary time shifts. If a reader says, "That's interesting, but what's it got to do with what's going on now?" chances are that time shift isn't needed.

5. DO I NEED A TIME SHIFT THAT'S NOT YET HERE?

Finally, you need to consider what's missing. Is there some crucial scene that you've not yet shown? Through the eight pages of "Wild Horses," for example, I've moved both forward and backward in time, until the reader learns, on page 7 in scene Q (found on page 253 of this book), just how important the wild horses are to both William and Althea's relationship and to his feelings about that relationship. I couldn't have revealed this information earlier, as it's only now that William is becoming aware of how it's tied up with his feelings about Althea's Alzheimer's disease. But, if I'd merely moved chronologically from Thelma Cheskie offering more coffee (scene P) to the final section (scenes S, T, and U), the story's emotional impact would have been depleted.

It's time shifts like this that, in the end, can make the difference for fictions, offering a last transcendent moment to make them shine.

MINDING YOUR STORY
Time Management

Look at a fiction you love and have read a number of times. (If you haven't read a fiction you love more than once, now is the time to acquire that practice. It's part of learning to read as a writer.) You should be familiar enough with this fiction that you can answer the following questions either from memory or by simply flipping quickly through its pages.

1. Where in time does the fiction begin?
2. Why do you think the fiction begins here?
3. What would be lost if the fiction began at a different time?
4. Can you think of a way the emotional impact of the fiction might be *improved* if the fiction began at a different point in time?

Now, take out a fiction you are working on but are not yet satisfied with. Very quickly, in much the same way you worked with the fiction above, answer the same questions for your own fiction. It won't be as easy as it was for someone else's work, at least not at first. Ultimately, though, looking at your own fiction this way will help you begin to revise and rewrite it with an eye towards managing its time effectively.

If the second part of this exercise seems impossible to you, you might consider asking someone you trust in your writers' group to answer these questions of your work. Those insights may give you the jump-start you need to learn how to improve your fiction's pacing on your own.

chapter 13
TENSE AND TENSION

I'm not here to teach you the difference between past, present, and future tenses (or all the subjunctive, imperative, and auxiliary tenses in between). For that, I recommend a good grammar book. My favorite is Strunk and White's *The Elements of Style*.

That said, two things about tense are worth mentioning as we conclude our discussion of pacing:

1. Pick one tense and stick with it.
2. Think of tense in terms of *kairos*—holy time—rather than *chronos*—clock time.

Playing With Tenses

True or false? Deciding whether to use past or present tense throughout a fiction is an arbitrary choice.

If you've learned anything about my approach to writing fiction, you already know my answer: No decision you make in your writing is arbitrary, and the same holds true for the tense you use to tell your tale. Naturally, there are advantages and disadvantages whether you're using past or present tense, so the choice you make will either aid your fiction or make your job more difficult.

Present tense offers a sense of immediacy. Within its no-nonsense, journalistic recitation of events, the reader feels in the moment, learns each eventuality along with the point-of-view character, and never knows what's coming next until it happens. There's a Hemingway-esque terseness to present tense, a "just the facts, ma'am" minimalism that hasn't got time to look or consider beneath the surface.

Present tense is limited by these advantages, however: There's never a moment to get behind or ahead of the fiction because we're moving in time with it, and so we can't get deeper, closer to the fiction's heart. A number of contemporary writers disdain present-tense narratives for this very reason: Lynne Sharon Schwartz, novelist and author of the memoir *Ruined by Reading*, for example, calls it a device that allows the writer to skirt what really matters in a fiction.

Past tense offers you space in which to explore both your characters and story more closely. It's understood that what's being told now has already happened, so you can employ both flashback and flash-forward (characters' imaginings and musings), as well as use foreshadowing and hindsight more effectively, all without taking the reader out of the story. At the same time, however, the reader is a step removed from the story.

PRESENT TENSE

PLUSSES	MINUSES
sense of immediacy, in the moment with point-of-view character, terse, direct	no narrative distance, lack of depth, no "heart"

PAST TENSE

PLUSSES	MINUSES
room to move around in time, flashbacks and flash-forwards, foreshadowing and hindsight	sense of removal from story

FROM PRESENT TO PAST

Nothing shows how the use of tense works better than examples, so here's a paragraph from my novel *Dissonance*. The first example represents the way the text is written, in present tense:

I am a piano teacher. Monday through Friday afternoons, from three-thirty until six, I entertain children in various stages of their movement toward adulthood with the mysteries of the instrument. My Steinway Grand sits in a plant-filled room with good, filtered southern light, and in winter as the shadows lengthen, the plants etch mottled patterns across both the keys and the faces of the young students. The keys are white and black; the students are white—Anglo, as we call them here—and the shadows are a translucent grey that border on an illusion. When the shadows surrender to the dark, I turn on the single focused light above the music stand, its glare causing momentary blinking in the student. "Again," I say, as if I have not noticed the darkness, as if I have not noticed the way a sudden spotlight can startle a living creature into stillness.

Now, I've taken the same paragraph and changed it into past tense.

I was a piano teacher. Monday through Friday afternoons, from three-thirty until six, I entertained children in various stages of their movement toward adulthood with the mysteries of the instrument. My Steinway Grand sat in a plant-filled room with good, filtered southern light, and in winter as the shadows lengthened, the plants etched mottled patterns across both the keys and the faces of the young students. The keys were white and black; the students were white …

There's no need to go on; from the first sentence in the second example, everything changes. There's a sense of reminiscent narrator, for one thing, and it seems the narrator is no longer doing these things or living in this place. Part of this is voice, of course. But it's mostly tense. The *kairos* of the first paragraph's immediacy is lost when the tense is switched from present to past.

FROM PAST TO PRESENT

Of course, the opposite holds true as well, and turning a past-tense narrative into a present-tense one will do it a similar disservice. Here's another example from *Dissonance*:

> While my father showed Paul his roses, I walked down the path to the canyon's edge. It was June, a hot month, but a coolness seemed to rise from the chasm, and a pair of hawks floated lazily at the level of my eyes. On the far side of the canyon, new houses were sprouting in a subdivision—aluminum-sided ranches surrounded by the stumps of the ponderosas razed to make room for them.
>
> This was during the uranium boom, when enterprising businessmen grouped together and leased land from the Indian tribes, then hired cheap Indian labor to dig the ore out. Uranium was everywhere in the four-states region, a coincidence whose providence was not lost on my father, who was one of the men getting rich.

Now, that same passage, rewritten in present tense:

> While my father shows Paul his roses, I walk down the path to the canyon's edge. It is June, a hot month, but a coolness seems to rise from the chasm, and a pair of hawks floats lazily at the level of my eyes. On the far side of the canyon, new houses are sprouting in a subdivision—aluminum-sided ranches surrounded by the stumps of the ponderosas razed to make room for them.
>
> This is during the uranium boom, when enterprising businessmen group together and lease land from the Indian tribes, then hire cheap Indian labor to dig the ore out. Uranium is everywhere in the four-states region, a coincidence whose providence is not lost on my father, who is one of the men getting rich.

When these two paragraphs are switched to present tense, the opening paragraph feels all right at first, but the additional information provided at the end of the first paragraph and throughout the second feels oddly out of step with the narrative. The information floats (like those hawks) rather than being grounded in the narrative as it is when I use past tense. For the narrative voice to ring true in the second paragraph, I had to employ past tense throughout this passage.

ROOM TO WORK (AND PLAY)

You may have noted that I broke my first rule when I was writing *Dissonance*: I didn't pick one tense and stick with it. *Dissonance* is a multithreaded narrative, and I used tense very intentionally throughout to achieve and maintain tension. I learned how to do this by studying a number of masters: Penelope Lively, Alice Munro, Carol Shields, and Ian McEwan, to name but four. If you want to use tense to achieve tension, learning from your own masters is the best method I know.

But there's a difference between working (and playing) with tense and sloppy writing that slips back and forth between tenses. Writers who play with tense understand the way they ought to work before they begin to use them to their advantage. Editors and readers can spot this difference immediately, and so should you, the craftsperson. As with all aspects of fiction writing, mastering the basics will allow you to use them in new and exciting ways.

Picking one tense and sticking with it is the number one rule. Rule two is to consider how the tense you're using makes the fiction feel. Remember that *kairos* refers to a fiction's emotional time, so this is intimately tied to its *kairos*. The wrong tense can entirely change the feel of a fiction, so changing tense may be just the thing your fiction's been looking for.

Lastly, when you do decide to change the tense of a fiction, be aware that it will require far more than merely changing the verbs. It's often best to rewrite rather than simply revise if you decide to change tense. I'll discuss this in far more depth in Part III, when I talk about revision and rewriting.

MINDING YOUR STORY
Working With Tenses

Pick a paragraph from a fiction you love. The masters (Hemingway, Didion, Porter) work particularly well for this exercise, but any fiction will serve to illustrate. Once you pick a paragraph, use your computer's word processing program to rewrite the paragraph in its opposite tense—past if it's currently in present, present if it's currently in past.

How did this alteration change the feel of the paragraph? It should be immediately obvious whether a sense of immediacy (present) or retrospection (past) is lost, but if this exercise doesn't work for a particular paragraph, try it again with another.

Now, try the same thing with a paragraph of your own from a fiction you know isn't working. (It's preferable if you haven't yet ascertained *why* it isn't working.) As noted above, you will need to do more than merely change the verb tense when you decide to change tenses in a fiction, but this exercise may at least alert you to the possibility that a change in tense is just what your fiction needs.

chapter 14
WHO DO YOU LOVE?

Sure, this is a book about writing, but in this chapter I'd like to talk about reading. More specifically, I'd like to talk about *your* reading, and what it can teach you about writing.

First, you should know that I'm a particular and demanding reader. That's because I read as a writer, which means something can't merely work for me, I have to figure out why it works. In this chapter, you'll learn to read as a writer, too, which includes looking both at the lines and between them in order to figure out the *why* of writing that leaves you begging for more.

Master Class

I'm sure by now you know some of the writers I consider my own masters: Katherine Anne Porter, Alice Munro, Carol Shields, Joan Didion, to name but a few. I know they're my masters because every time I read and reread their work, I ask myself again what it is about their writing that makes such a strong connection with me as a reader.

Now, let me broaden this a bit so it applies to you, as well. My questions are often about writing that connects, because that's my thing—connecting with readers. Yes, I also look at language, a story's mind and structure, the details, the characters, and, and, and. But ultimately, I adore the writers I do because again and again they connect with me. And that's what I want to do in my own writing—connect.

Now, what you're looking for may (no, *will*) be quite different from what I seek. This means that a writer I love may leave you cold—and vice versa—or that you may love the same writer, but for a different reason. I think the world would be a very dull place if we all loved the same things, so I don't expect you to have the same masters (although I'll be delighted if you do). What this means, though, is that the first thing to consider when it comes to reading as a writer is what writers you already love. Take a moment to do that now.

FINDING YOUR OWN MASTERS

While each of your masters may have more than one thing to teach you, the next step is to find the commonality amongst them. So, for each of the writers that you love, consider why their writing resonates for you. Let's say, for example, that you picked Isabel Allende, Annie Dillard, and Sue Miller. I would say immediately that all three of these writers are first of all storytellers, which suggests that's what you hope to do with your own fiction, too. This brings us to the next question: How does each of them tell a story?

I won't answer this question here, first of all because your favorite writers will likely be different and, second, because answering it regarding your own masters is part of learning to read as writer. What I can do, however, is explore how my own masters connect with me.

WORKING WITH MY MASTERS

One of the things I've noticed is that many of my favorite writers combine two sophisticated techniques, stream of consciousness and authorial intrusion, to work their magic. Both of these methods are particularly conducive to creating a story with a mind of its own that connects with readers, which is why I consider these writers my masters.

The next question, however, is *how* do they do these things. For this I need to dig more deeply into their methodologies.

STREAM OF CONSCIOUSNESS

In the short story "The Jilting of Granny Weatherall," Katherine Anne Porter wields her trademark "stream of consciousness," in which the reader is so far inside the character's mind that it appears there is no author at all. To illustrate, here is the beginning of that classic:

> She flicked her wrist neatly out of Doctor Harry's pudgy careful fingers and pulled the sheet up to her chin. That brat ought to be in knee breeches. Doctoring around the country with spectacles on his nose! "Get along now, take your schoolbooks and go. There's nothing wrong with me."

You'll immediately note that this is a third-person narrative ("she"), which you may believe is at cross purposes with a stream-of-consciousness narrative, where the reader is immersed in one character's mind. But in fact, this third-person point of view serves Porter's purpose doubly well: It means she'll be able to intrude herself when she wants, without the reader feeling jarred, because Porter has established Granny's voice so thoroughly that the story seems entirely in her point of view.

Finally, the epiphany to which Porter builds necessitates a narrative distancing that separates character and narrator. So, while contemporary readers don't expect a separate, omniscient narrator, in the case of stream-of-consciousness, it seems to me to add a much-needed dimension that's lost with a first- or third-person limited narration.

MOVING AROUND IN TIME

Another method all of my masters are, well, masters of, is moving around within the mind of a story. Here is an example from "Friend of My Youth," by Alice Munro. The narrator is considering a woman she once knew, named Flora.

> But I have thought of her since. I have wondered what kind of store ...
>
> (Or) She might meet a man. A friend's widowed brother, perhaps...
>
> I might go into a store and find her.
>
> No, no. She would be dead a long time now.
>
> But suppose I had gone into a store – perhaps a department store ... I imagine her listening ...
>
> Of course, it's my mother I'm thinking of, my mother as she was in those dreams, saying, It's nothing, just this little tremor; saying it with such astonishing lighthearted forgiveness, Oh, I knew you'd come someday ...

I've left a lot out, to show you as much as I could about the way Munro moves around a story. After the astonishing section partially quoted above, in which the narrator imagines running into Flora, imagines a conversation with her (but, "No, no. She would be dead a long time now."), then realizes that "it's really [her] mother [she's] thinking of," Munro inserts one of her trademark line breaks, and then ends the story with a paragraph about the Cameronians.

That paragraph (I've not included it) seems to hang, separate, alone. What's it about? Why is it there? The answer is that it's authorial intrusion at its finest and most bald-faced, and the last line of this marvelous story reads, "One of their ministers, in a mood of firm rejoicing at his own hanging, excommunicated all the other preachers in the world." Not only does this line shed light on the quite different story that came before, it *changes* it. Without this authorial intrusion, in other words, the story exists on one less level than it does with it there.

But I can't do Alice Munro justice here. My advice: Read her, and read her again.

LIFETIMES ON THE HEADS OF PINS

Like Munro, my favorite writers share an ability to move all over the place in time while the narrative hangs in a single moment. While I've covered this extensively already, an example here will show you how I studied one of my masters to learn how she did it. This is Carol Shields's *Unless*. The characters in this scene are having dinner with a man whose wife has recently left him, and who has been talking about the theory of relativity:

> The theory of relativity would not bring Colin's wife hurrying back to the old stone house on Oriole Parkway. It would not bring my daughter Norah home from the corner of Bathurst and Bloor, or the Promise Hostel where she beds at night. Tom and I followed her one day; we had to know how she managed, whether she was safe. The weather would be turning cold soon. How does she bear it? Cold concrete. Dirt. Uncombed hair.

"Would you say," I asked Colin—I had not spoken for several minutes— "that the theory of relativity has reduced the weight of goodness and depravity in the world?"

Note how, using parallel construction (in this case, clauses naming places), the narrator leaves the table and thinks about her daughter, who has left college to sit at a Toronto subway entrance holding a sign that reads, "goodness." And note how the narrator skewers the speaker and his theories when she returns to the story's present. This sudden shift in the characters' interactions is earned via the direction and intent of the point-of-view character's thoughts. I like to think of such moments as lifetimes on the heads of pins.

Read It Again

Just because you already have a handful of masters to teach you doesn't mean you shouldn't constantly be seeking more. It's simple to do this: Whenever you read something that knocks your socks off, read it again. Ask yourself questions about the writing, such as:

+ Why does this astonish me?
+ What is it about this writing that speaks to me?

These questions aren't as easy as they sound. It's easy to say you love Ernest Hemingway for his terseness or Jeffrey Eugenides for his exuberance. What you need to do as a writer, though, is dig deeper. Yes, Hemingway's writing may appear terse, but the way he arranges his deceptively short words and sentences are why they pack such a whammy. And yes, Jeffrey Eugenides's writing is an absolute joy to read partly because it was clearly such a joy for him to write, but the cumulative total of what he writes adds up to much more than the mere parts, because of the details that he chooses and the way he reveals them.

CHANNELING YOUR MASTERS

I know what you're thinking: Not only is she from New Mexico and the co-author of all those New Age Idiot's Guides, now she's going to try to tell me to channel my masters. Well, don't worry about getting your Ouija board out quite yet (unless, that is, you want to).

What I mean when I say "channel your masters," is to allow yourself to feel their words in your own hand. That's right: Copy the words in your own handwriting. Not only will this help you feel the author's particular rhythms, you'll become more aware of the words she or he uses, the way she or he arranges them, how they sound, how they feel. In addition, you'll become attuned to punctuation, sentence length, tense, and paragraphing.

It's always very hard for me to stop typing my masters' words when I'm working on a column, book, or class (as now), but in fact, one of the ways

I've learned from each of them is to copy out whole sections of their work in my own handwriting. While you may worry that such an exercise is imitative, it turns out that practicing your favorites' rhythms ultimately helps you to find your own as well.

Reading as a Writer

Once you begin to read as a writer, it's hard to go back to reading as a reader. This is a hard, sad truth, and if you prefer to read as a reader, you may have to reconsider your future as a writer. (I'm serious.) I am unable to read anything, whether it's a short story, a magazine article, or a cereal box, without considering the way the words fit together on the page (or cardboard, as the case may be).

Reading as a writer means that whenever something you read wows you, it's not enough to say *wow*: You must figure out why. Is it the way the words fit together on the page? The characters or their interactions? The turns of plot? The movement in time or stream of consciousness? The way you can't put the book down? How does the author make that happen? How? How? How?

All this said, I think there are a number of things all writers should consider as they study with their masters:

+ the way words fit together on the page
+ characters and their interactions
+ turns of plot
+ I couldn't put it down-ness

Let's look at each of these briefly, so I can show you why I think they're so important.

THE WAY THE WORDS FIT TOGETHER ON THE PAGE

You may recall Joan Didion's discussion of the beginning of *A Farewell to Arms* in chapter nine. Parsing a master's work in this way is a telling exercise for a number of reasons. First of all, it suggests how you might take apart a piece of writing that amazes you. But to me, even more important is the reminder that a writer of Didion's caliber is moved to do this, that just like us, Didion is constantly seeking to learn from her masters.

I encourage you to follow Didion's example whenever you read something that stuns, amazes, or otherwise startles you. Count the words, the number of syllables in each word, the instances of "the" and "and," as Didion does. Like Didion, consider the placement of each comma and period, and why the author chose to place them (or not place them) where they are. Pay attention to the length and rhythm of each sentence, just as the best writers do, over and over again, and soon, just as it has for your masters, these conscious decisions will become automatic in your own fiction, as well.

CHARACTERS AND THEIR INTERACTIONS

Literary fiction, which is my own preference, is character-driven (as opposed to more plot-driven commercial fiction), so the way characters both act and interact is something I not only desire from writing I love, it is something I expect. To say that I have no patience with the wooden, stereotypical characters who populate commercial fiction is a severe understatement: I read only a few pages of *The DaVinci Code* before taking it back to the library in disgust because I found the characters so one-dimensional and wooden. (My husband keeps begging me to put these prejudices aside and write just one commercial book. Would that I could!)

If your fiction begins with character rather than plot, as I suggested in Part I, your book is far more likely to not only have characters who live and breathe on the page, but also to interest a smart, demanding reader like me. (Of course, if you're in it just for the money, you could be studying with the wrong master!)

TURNS OF PLOT

While plot-driven fiction, where character is secondary, isn't my cup of tea, I nonetheless am a huge fan of a cadre of mystery writers who write brilliantly well. To name but a few: Sara Paretsky, Marica Muller, and Kate Atkinson utterly amaze me with their ability to not only bring characters alive on the page, but to keep those pages turning because of turns of plot. The lesson here is not to limit yourself to one genre when you are seeking masters, particularly if you know you have a weakness in a specific area.

I COULDN'T PUT IT DOWN-NESS

Actually, I call this *Lonesome Dove*-itis, and for those of you who were similarly affected when you first read this Larry McMurtry masterpiece, the term needs no further definition. For those who somehow missed the book (I suppose it's possible you weren't yet born when the book came out, which depresses the hell out of me), however, it turns out that what McMurtry did to keep readers turning pages far into the night was amazingly simple.

First, he had two (and at times, more) equally compelling narrative threads running at the same time. At the end of each chapter, the reader wanted to keep reading to find out what happened next. But when she turned the page, she was back in the other narrative, the one she'd wanted to find out about when she'd turned the page after the end of the previous chapter. Back and forth between Gus and July, I compulsively turned those pages. So, in fact, did my husband. Though we'd only recently begun dating at the time, I'd left the book on his coffee table, thinking he might like it. He did like it. In fact, when he finished it, he called to tell me he hated me (hardly something one wants to hear when you've first started seeing someone). It turned out the book had kept him up all night (and he didn't really hate me after all).

MINDING YOUR STORY
Reading as a Writer

This exercise is really a simple reiteration of the various methods I've suggested throughout this chapter.

1. Think about who your favorite writers are, the ones you read over and over. What do they have in common?
2. What about that commonality do you hope to emulate in your own writing?
3. How does each of your masters do what he or she does?
4. When you read something that knocks your socks off, read it again.
5. Ask yourself questions about the writing: Why does this astonish me? What is it about this writing that speaks to me?
6. Copy your masters' words in your own handwriting to feel the authors' rhythms. Note the words the authors use, the way they arrange them, how the words sound, how they feel. Note their use of punctuation, sentence length, tense, paragraphing.
7. And then, go back and read it again.

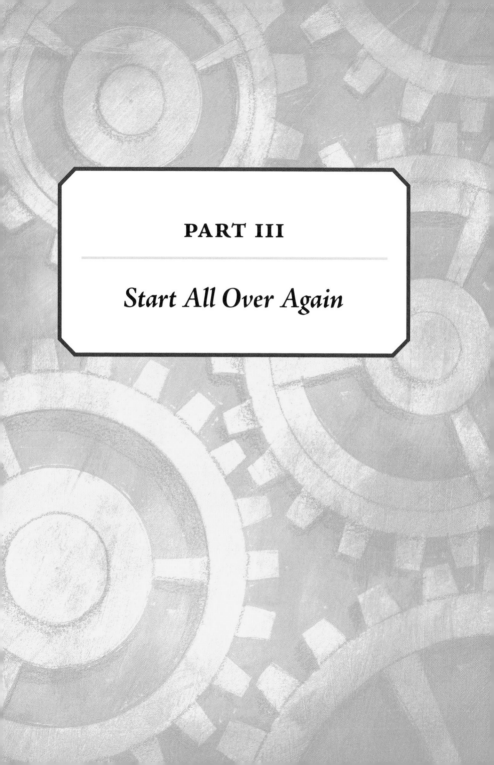

PART III

Start All Over Again

chapter 15
START ALL OVER AGAIN

There are few more satisfying moments in a fiction-writing life than when you type "The End" on a manuscript. Sure, there may be one or two (or more) niggles in your mind about certain passages, but you're—hallelujah!—finished, right?

Wrong.

What I've discovered in the many years I've been doing this is that the still more satisfying moments are yet to come—when I return to the material and start all over again. In this last section of *The Mind of Your Story*, I'll talk about my methods of revision and rewriting, to me the most gratifying—and most difficult—aspect of crafting a work of fiction that connects with readers.

Before we begin, however, I'd like to point out yet again that my methods and yours will most likely differ in some ways. It is my hope that in showing you my own way of working, step by step by step, you'll come to discover the process of writing—and rewriting—your own fiction that works best for you.

All Done? Now Put It in the Closet

You should think of rewriting and revision as opportunities you give yourself to make your manuscript more closely resemble the fiction you imagine. But, that said, resist the urge to begin rewriting the moment you finish writing. Doing this won't work for a number of reasons: First, because you're still too close to the material, and second, because editorial left brain can make creative right brain doubt every word she ever wrote.

So, how long should you wait before you begin rewriting? To the horror of many of my older students, I like to quote Homer, who suggested waiting seven years after the completion of the first draft before beginning to revise. I don't know how Homer came up with that magic number, but I do know he was on to something, because the best thing you can do after you type "The End" is print the sucker out and *put it away*. I put *my* manuscripts into notebooks that I keep in my office's closet, hence my phrase, "Put it in the closet."

THE "OOPS" FACTOR

Yes, your first impulse will likely be to find the fattest envelope you can and send your fresh-printed manuscript to every agent whose last name begins with "A." On behalf of those agents (and their hardworking assistants), I beseech you: Don't.

Why? Because not only will you discover that egregious error on page 7 when you get home from the post office, but you'll realize the next morning (or, perhaps, when you can't fall asleep that night) that if you begin instead on your current page 30, your plot will unfold far more effectively. And why, you'll lament the next afternoon, did you include that scene with Alice and Allen in the armory? Even your (nonwriting) spouse gently suggested that it did nothing for your story. And didn't you mean to add a scene after Allen discovers Amory and Alice in the armoire? You wrote yourself a note to do so, but somehow, you must have forgotten. And now the manuscript is on its way to Almost, Anon., and Adios.

Of course you're eager to share your magnum opus with the world. But once an agent or editor has rejected it, you don't get a second chance with him or her (except for that extremely rare instance where someone writes back and suggests that if you do A, B, and C, he'll take another look). Do you really want to blow your chances by sending your manuscript right this minute, without some time to consider—and reconsider—it? I didn't think so.

If you have trusted readers, or if you're in a writing workshop, of course, go ahead and share it with them. (I'll look at writing workshops in depth in chapter eighteen.) Otherwise, I beseech you, print out a copy and then *put it away*. This symbolic act will help you put the project out of your mind, too, and that's equally important. For the next few weeks (at the least) and several years (at the best), you're not going to consciously think about this book. Either you'll move on to the next one or give yourself a break. After all, you've earned it.

But! But! But!

Sorry, no buts allowed. In fact, I've anticipated your buts, and here are my rebuttals.

"IT'S STILL CALLING TO ME"

If you've put your manuscript "in the closet" but are nonetheless still enraptured by your story, can't get your characters out of your head, wake up with the urge to write more, or otherwise want to continue to climb back inside your fiction, the message is that your draft isn't yet finished (that "The End" to the contrary), and you shouldn't have put it in the closet in the first place. Fictions that aren't close to being finished are the ones that wake us up in the middle of the night. Fictions that need time to percolate will leave us alone.

"I EDIT AS I GO"

Me, too. But the difference between cleaning up a close-to-finished manuscript and fixing a broken one comes back to understanding the art of fiction. Here, we arrive full circle, back to the first two parts of this book, chapters that explored everything from your fiction's origins to character, plot, setting, point of view, pacing, and voice. If you haven't mastered these basics, their lack will be apparent in your draft. If you have, you'll know when a manuscript needs to spend more time in your closet before it's ready for a re-look.

"I MAY BE DEAD IN TWO MONTHS"

If you truly know you have a limited time to live, first of all, my sincere condolences. Obviously, this advice will not apply when time is of the essence. I would suggest an outside editor to jump-start the revision process, if that's the case.

If, however, you're just invoking this as a fatalistic possibility, sorry. I stand by my adage to let your manuscript percolate.

What Do I Do While My Manuscript Is Percolating?

You write.

In fact, ideally, when you put one manuscript in the closet, you'll take another out, so of course it's to your advantage to have as many drafts as possible. There are a number of good reasons for this. First of all, knowing that you are writing a *draft* frees you to simply get the fiction down the first time (and incidentally also does a great deal to keep that master stalker of writers, procrastination, away). Second, putting all those drafts in the closet means they're there waiting for you to begin revising when another joins them.

But before discussing what will come out of the closet, let's look at what happens when I put a manuscript in my closet (as I did this past week). First, I give myself a reward. These rewards are always little things, but they give me great pleasure. Sometimes I just get in my car and drive somewhere I've never been. Once I bought myself a great pair of cowboy boots that I still wear often. Another time I went to a used bookstore in Albuquerque and spent the whole afternoon just browsing.

Of course, these simple pleasures may not be your thing. You can, and should, reward yourself however you like. The secret to a reward system that works is to pick little things that will give *you* a lot of pleasure. I think it helps if you don't ordinarily indulge yourself, and it helps even more if you chained yourself to your desk during the months it took to get that draft finished, so that an outing means something. That's basically what I do.

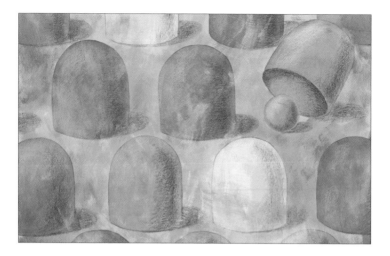

PICKING WHAT'S NEXT

But the day after I receive my reward, it's back to work. I'd love to tell you that there's a method to my madness, that I keep a spreadsheet that tells me when each draft has gone into the closet in the first place so I know which one is ready to take out again. Wouldn't that be organized and efficient? Would that it were true. Instead, I rely on instinct to tell me what's ready for revision.

So when I return to my closet to select a manuscript to begin revising, without a spreadsheet to guide me, how do I know which manuscript to take out of the closet? (By the way, there's nothing wrong with using a spreadsheet to keep track of what went in the closet when; it's just not something that works for me.) The answer is that it's a gut thing. I just know.

IT'S WHAT YOU KNOW

Let me explain via an analogy not only why I put so much faith in these intuitive systems but why I think they work. I'm sure you've had the experience of picking up a book everyone else is raving about, only to find it holds absolutely no interest for you. But then, two, five, or even ten years later, you'll pick that same book up and not be able to put it down. What gives?

As you well know, there's nothing quite like the right book at the right time (except, perhaps, the wrong book at the wrong time). Everything about it resonates for you, because the book forges a connection with the place you are in your life. This same principal applies to knowing which manuscript it's time to start working on again. If you make a false start, you'll know almost at once, just as you do with that book. It doesn't mean the false-start manuscript isn't worth working on; it's simply not the manuscript you should be working on *now*.

When you select the right manuscript, however, you'll feel more and more excited as you read it. You'll see what you were trying to do, but at the same time you'll also be able to see how rewriting and revision will make the manuscript still stronger.

And that's the main thing: Coming back to a manuscript that's percolated for a while should be *exciting*. If you don't put a manuscript away for awhile—if you revisit it immediately—the freshness of rediscovery is lost. Instead, it's just the same thing, yet again, something to be slogged through rather than an opportunity for rediscovery (as well as the discovery of gifts you gave yourself without even being aware of them).

Here's an example of such a "gift": In a friend's manuscript, when a man goes to see his ex-wife, he has flowers in his car. As they aren't for her, he keeps fiddling with them to keep them out of her line of vision. But what if, instead, she sees them, and asks if they are for her? The answer is this not-yet-finished scene might then move to the next level via the exchange that ensues.

TIME TO SEE WHAT'S BETWEEN THE LINES

What happens during the percolation period is so important to the overall success of your book that if you skip it, chances are your book will never move from okay to outrageous. With the excitement of rediscovery comes the opportunity to polish a draft into something truly special. How? There are so many big issues to address, the next four chapters are devoted to them.

Of course, if you're happy with just okay, that's fine. Not every writer is the raging perfectionist I am. Right now, I have four novels and six short stories in my own closet, each needing a "something more" I haven't yet discerned. In other words, even writers who've grasped the basics know it takes time for a fiction to reveal itself—not just the time it takes to write it the first time, but *the time for what's hidden between the words to reveal itself.* And that, finally, is why you don't want to dash madly to the finish: You may miss the most important thing you'll ever write, the heart of the matter, the thing that compelled you to begin in the first place.

You, the Writer, vs. You, the Editor

Once again, I urge you to remember that writing and rewriting are two very different things, so different that they involve discrete areas of the brain: Your right brain creates; your left brain edits.

Ideally, you should keep these two aspects of yourself separate. If you don't, you may find yourself doing what one of my students did. Every time she wrote a new sentence, she'd immediately read it, pronounce it awful, and rewrite it. Then she'd read the new sentence and rewrite that. No wonder she never finished an assignment, let alone a short story!

What that student was doing was allowing her editor (left brain) to get in the way of her creator (right brain). This slow and meticulous method of writing may have worked for Flaubert (or maybe not; look at how little he left us), but it's something I strongly discourage, mainly because it hampers the creative side of you until, finally, your creative side gives up. Nonetheless, it's a common occurrence, probably because it arises, at least in part, from when we were kids and were told to clean up our messes.

MAKING A MESS

What you should do instead is go ahead and make a mess, and worry about cleaning it up later. Resist the "parent" in your head who's telling you to clean it up now. That parent needs to get out, not just of your head, but of the room, until you get to the revision and rewriting part.

Then, rather than worrying what your internal parent will say, whenever you feel the urge, *just write*. Don't worry about spelling, grammar, sentence structure, paragraphing, how it looks or sounds, or even what your parents, children, spouse, or friends (or enemies) will think. In this creative right-brain stage, you are simply getting it all down on paper. Thanks to the wonder of computers, you'll be able to go back again (and again and again) and fiddle with what you create later. In short, don't stop to analyze. Don't stop at all—until you get to the revision phase.

REVISION AND REWRITING

I like to delineate the difference between revision and rewriting thusly: In revision, you work with what you have, tweaking, moving things around, and subtly altering what you've written in order to polish it.

Rewriting, however, is far bigger, as it involves starting from scratch. I do a lot of rewriting. The novel I just finished, in fact, is the sixth *total* rewrite of material I first tackled over twenty years ago. With each version, I got a little closer to (or sometimes, I now see, farther from) what I want the novel to be. But because the novel covers a long period of time (half of the twentieth century), I needed to find a way to be close to the material without leaving enormous gaps of time in between. I think I've finally found a way to do that in my recent rewrite. (At least, I hope so …)

Even when you decide the material you have is worth keeping, you'll nonetheless have a lot of work to do in the revision department. Revision involves everything from deciding where your fiction begins to where each scene will work most effectively. In addition, revision is where you will cut those great swaths of narrative that don't belong in this particular fiction, as well as fill in the blanks you may or may not have realized you left. Revision, in other words, involves far more than using your word-processing program's thesaurus. It means looking at your fiction *as a whole* and then step-by-step tweaking and tugging it until you yourself say, "Wow! That's really good!"

MINDING YOUR STORY
Give Yourself a Gift

This chapter's exercise is designed to not only get you out of your workspace, but out of yourself. All that's required is that you think about some ways of rewarding yourself that will be both meaningful and long-lasting. Take your time considering what would make you happy. The best rewards don't have to cost much, and may or may not involve other people.

Now, the next time you finish a manuscript, go ahead and give yourself one of these rewards. After all, without bosses or peers to let you know what a great job you've done, the rewarding is up to you. Besides, you've earned it!

chapter 16
WHERE DO I BEGIN REVISING?

Revision can be a daunting task, especially if the project you're working on is a novel. It's easy to say you should start with the big stuff and move to the small, but when you sit down with your manuscript, it's hard to know where and how to begin. In this chapter, I'll help you break down the revision process into manageable tasks that will show not just what you need to do when you begin revising, but how to go about it.

The Editor Cometh

Let's say you've done as I suggested and written with abandon, with your editor safely tucked away. You've typed (hallelujah!) "The End" and printed out your manuscript, then put it in your closet for at least a month (and preferably longer). Finally, the day has arrived when you're ready to take the manuscript out of your closet in order to decide whether it will require revision or rewriting.

Now, the editor cometh, with his or her blue pencil. The editor, of course, is you, and "blue pencil" is one of the ways we refer to what an editor does, although the pencil no longer has to be blue, nor does it have to be a pencil. You may be in a writing group or have asked a few trusted others to read the manuscript and give you constructive feedback. But while other people's thoughts are helpful, the final arbiter—the final editor—on this go-round (on all go-rounds, actually) is you.

THE MARATHON READ-THROUGH

Today's the day. You open the closet. There's *The Great American Novel*. You forgot all about it. But now, it's time to read what you wrote. This is where the Marathon Read-Through comes in. First, make sure you have enough time to read the manuscript straight through without being interrupted. This is important: You want to have as much of your fiction in your head as possible, in order to catch those pesky repetitions and continuity errors.

Next, make yourself comfortable. Make sure you won't be interrupted. (Answering machine: check. Babysitter: check. Beverage of choice: check. Etc.) Keep a pen or pencil *in your hand*. (This will ensure you will write your thoughts on the manuscript rather than mull over them.) Of course, you may write as much or as little on your manuscript as you like. Now, start reading.

Oh my. Did I write that? What was I thinking? I write so much better than that now. Why did I ever imagine that was a good opening sentence? And that Allen! He's so, so alien! It's a good thing trash day's tomorrow …

But wait! Don't toss that manuscript! Instead, take heart from novelist Frank Yerby, who said, "a really good novel is made with a knife not a pen." It's the cutting (and filling in) that will make the difference between the book you just got out of the closet and, say, *The Great Gatsby*. But how will you, the creator of *The Great American Novel*, turn it from landfill fodder to gold?

The answer is that left brain will do the editing. This is one of the main reasons it's so important to put the manuscript away for a while: You don't want to threaten your creative side with the much harsher realities of what your editorial side will suggest.

ENTER LEFT BRAIN, SMIRKING

When left brain shows up, it's time to send right brain out for a haircut or, better yet, a massage. Left brain isn't going to pat you on the back and tell you how wonderful you are, oh no. Left brain's going to tell you, in no uncertain terms, that you suck. Left brain is going to see that sentence you thought was the most gorgeous thing you'd ever written and tell you it's a candidate for the Worst Thing Ever Done With a Computer Award.

It's easy to hate left brain. For one thing, it's got no time for niceties like the people in your writing workshop, who will always tell you what they love about your fiction before they (gently) suggest how you might improve it. Nope. Left brain cuts right to the chase, to the heart of the matter, and to your heart of hearts. *Who the heck do you think you are?* left brain's going to ask. *You can't get away with this. I simply won't allow it.* And so on and so forth, until you feel like the rabbits in my yard do when the dogs come dashing out: quivery and alone.

PAY ATTENTION TO THOSE INTUITIVE NUDGES

What left brain's really doing, though, is translating a decidedly right-brain thing: It's paying attention to your intuitive nudges. In fact, it's likely that even as you wrote that glorious sentence, something nagged at the back of your mind. You decided to ignore it; it was just you, worrying, after all.

But our intuitive nudges aren't wrong. They "know" things in a way that has nothing to do with language, thinking, or logic, and they know when something isn't quite right. It's like walking into a room and smelling a smell that doesn't belong. You can ignore it, but that doesn't make it go away.

All too often, it's our very favorite clauses that are standing in the way of polished prose. There are two ways to look at this: One is that these phrases call attention to themselves and, so, pull the reader out of the narrative (so she can then put down your fiction and—uh-oh!—go to the bathroom). The other is that if they really are that good, then every other phrase in your fiction must be equally outstanding. Let me tell you, ma'am (and sir), that's a real tall order. If you feel you can live up to it, though, I heartily encourage you to do so. It's what I aim for, and believe me, it takes a lot of time. Still, I think it is worth doing, if it's what you want.

But other problems will prompt intuitive nudges, as well. You may not know yet what the problem is. If that's the case, simply flag the place the nudge "noojed" you, and then let it go. Left brain will let you know what's not working, so long as you're patient—and willing to listen once right brain has gotten the message.

Time to Sweat the Small Stuff

As you're doing your Marathon Read-Through, you might want to have a separate notebook for those flashes of inspiration that occur to you along the way. While this is something I seldom do myself, I probably should heed my own advice. I do, however, make a *lot* of notes directly on my manuscript. Let's begin by considering some of the little things your left brain (the editor) will notice that your right brain (the creator) would rather ignore.

I. DUMB MISTAKES

You may have changed a character's name and done a global search and replace (hereafter referred to as S&R), but if that name was misspelled or a nickname was used anywhere in the manuscript, S&R won't find it—and you won't see it—without some time away from the manuscript. Ditto homonyms (there, their, they're; its, it's; to, too, two). Even those of us who know the differences among these words make these mistakes, especially if we type fast. And ditto the wrong word entirely: Some of my own errors in this department have made me laugh out loud (but, thankfully, no one else—because I [mostly] caught them.) Finally, there those skipped words, most commonly verbs like the "are" I skipped earlier in this sentence. Time away from a manuscript means your rested eyes and no-longer-bored brain will be more likely to notice such boo-boos, while if you read the manuscript immediately after you finish writing it, you'll skip right over them because your mind supplies them.

2. CONTINUITY ERRORS

I've read far too many published books (and, of course, works-in-progress) where characters move impossibly from place to place, time to time, or worse, die on one page only to be mysteriously revived on the next. Another error I frequently see is a renamed character reverting to his or her original name, or changing names in the middle of the text.

All too often, this occurs in books by best-selling authors that are rushed into print without proper editing because of an eager public, in which case both author and editor are at fault. But—and here's the thing—these authors' first books (the ones that propelled them to best-seller status in the first place) didn't have such errors. If they had, they never would have been published. So it's up to you to make sure a character who's in a house in Kansas on one page doesn't end up in a strange land called Oz on the next, unless, of course, there's this tornado, see? And then …

3. SUPERFLUOUS SCENES

We all write them. In fact, they're often the best scenes we'll ever write. But all too often, *they don't belong in this fiction.* If you've put your manuscript in the closet for a month or longer, you'll see this much more clearly. You don't need to throw these scenes away, but you do need to get them out of a manuscript where they don't belong. You know the ones I mean. You hope an editor will love them as much as you do and will want them in there even though they don't belong. Not gonna happen. Get them out. Now.

4. MISSING SCENES

Narrative is not scene. Alluding to the murder that's the key to your book in a narrative sentence such as, "Later, when Larry learned Laura had killed Lance with a lariat, he laid the law on her," kills your chances of being published faster than Laura's lariat. *There is no substitute for a necessary scene.* None. If you can't write a particular scene because it's too close to your heart, too gory, too sexy, or too difficult, you are writing the wrong book.

When you come back to your manuscript after a time away, however, the absence of those scenes you'd convinced yourself you could skip over will look like walls from which pictures have been removed: What's missing will be all too obvious. The good news is that when you finally sit down to write these scenes, they'll be worth the effort.

5. TRUNCATED SCENES

The same holds true for scenes that suddenly end just as they reach the top of their narrative arc. Sometimes a phone or doorbell rings to rescue your character(s) from the climactic moment. Sometimes you simply end the scene at what seems its high point because it seems so, well, dramatic. But truncated scenes are immediately apparent to both professional and amateur readers because they feel incomplete.

It's not easy to "mine the ore," as writer Sydney Lea calls it. The work isn't simply dirty, it's going to dredge up a lot of tough stuff you worked very hard to bury. That's why we resist going there by ending our scenes too early (or even not writing them in the first place). But the best writing—the writing that will ultimately connect most strongly with readers—occurs when this ore is mined, when you expose those things you've hidden from yourself.

Think back to the Macauley and Lanning definition of fiction with which I began: "Fiction originates in direct personal impression linked by imagination with the writer's resources of experience." Our resources of experience work two ways (well, more than two, but I'm talking about a specific application in this case): to teach us what to seek and to teach us what to avoid. And, in yet another of fiction writing's numerous paradoxes, in order to create writing that connects, you must return to the things you'd rather avoid and mine them for all they're worth.

It's not easy. But it's cheaper than therapy. Plus it works. Getting the hardest stuff onto the page is the best thing you can do for your fiction—and for yourself. Trust me. Finishing those truncated scenes may be the most cathartic exercise you'll ever do.

6. DOT THOSE *IS*. CROSS THOSE *TS*.

The Marathon Read-Through is not the time to rely on self-help mantras. In fact, this is one of those instances when you *should* sweat the small stuff, such as the following:

CHANGE WORDS AND PHRASES

Sometimes this is simple, changing "mind" to "brain," say. But other times, more is needed. If a better word or phrase occurs to me at the moment I'm circling one that doesn't feel right, I pen it in. Otherwise, I simply note "something else" on the manuscript and move on. This is, after all, only the first of many times I'll be rereading this fiction. The important thing is to pay attention to every intuitive nudge and note it on your manuscript.

DELETE EXTRANEOUS REPETITIONS

In the throes of first-draftiness, we don't always realize we've used the word "use" three times in the same paragraph. A Marathon Read-Through alerts us to these repetitions. So that I don't slow my read-through by considering alternative words or phrases, I simply circle the offenders to revisit when I begin working with the manuscript on my computer, unless, as I've already mentioned, something occurs to me in the moment. If that's the case, I write it down.

DELETE WORDS, SENTENCES, PARAGRAPHS

One of the reasons I no longer accept first-draft editing jobs is the number of six-hundred-plus page first-draft manuscripts that exist. Quite a few of these are well written, but, except in very rare cases, no editor or agent will look at a first novel that's over 100,000 words (in standard font, that's about 400 pages). Why? Because it's clear from the length that the writer hasn't learned how to cut the excess.

Sometimes there are simply extraneous words. In *On Writing*, Stephen King suggests deleting every adverb, for example. (It's a great idea.) I also recommend deleting most participles and participial clauses (-ing constructions). Phrases like, "Coming into the room, she opened the door," make no sense in terms of time and spell sloppy writing to an editor.

It's also useful to seek and destroy what I call "stage directions." These are places where you've delineated how your characters are moving around a room. Ultimately, if these actions aren't moving the narrative forward at the same time, they have no place in the fiction.

Finally, sometimes we just go on a bit too long. When editor-you cometh, she or he must be ruthless in both acknowledging where this occurs and then cutting the offending material.

MOVE WORDS, SENTENCES, PARAGRAPHS

Sometimes, reversing a sentence's clauses can increase its strength and effectiveness exponentially. (I do this a lot on students' manuscripts.) In my own work, I often notice that if I take a sentence from farther down the page (or a few pages before or after) and move it up or down, everything that follows becomes much stronger. Whenever I move something elsewhere, however, be it a word, sentence, paragraph, or pages (and yes, I do this, as well), I know that I will need to reread everything that comes before and after it again very carefully to make sure my transitions work seamlessly with the changes. Try this yourself. Simply moving a word, phrase, or sentence once or twice will convince you how much tighter your manuscript can become with this simple revision tool.

Now, Sweat the Big Stuff

Of course, revisiting your manuscript with an eye toward revision involves much more than all those little things I've outlined above. With that in mind, here are some of the bigger things I do during a Marathon Read-Through.

WRITE NOTES TO MYSELF IN THE MARGIN

Here are some examples of notes I write to myself:

"c/f earlier ref W"   This Lisa-ese translates to "cross-reference to earlier reference to W," and means that I've found a connection worth making more explicit in some way.

"doesn't work"	Self-explanatory.
"cut?"	I'm not always convinced something needs to be cut, but nine times out of ten, if I make this note, the material ultimately ends up deleted.
"finish scene"	As I noted in number 5, ending a scene just before its emotional high point is fine in a first draft, but you need to acknowledge and finish these truncated scenes during your Marathon Read-Through.

NOTE WHAT-IFS THAT OCCUR TO ME AS I READ

Because I don't like to slow down my Marathon Read-Through with extensive revision and rewriting, I will make some notes in the margins when what-ifs that I haven't developed occur to me while I'm reading, such as, "What if W doesn't go to this meeting?" or "What if X is introduced here?" or "What if L & P are combined into one character?" Get the idea?

PUT STARS WHERE MORE IS NEEDED

Whether there are incomplete scenes or scenes that can be made stronger by expansion, what I do during this step is similar to the above what-ifs. Without slowing down, I write myself quick notes about possible scene resolutions, or, if nothing occurs to me, I simply write, "more needed here."

NOTE POSSIBLE MOVING OF
SECTIONS AND CHAPTERS ELSEWHERE

All too frequently during a Marathon Read-Through, I will at some point realize that moving entire scenes and chapters will have an enormous impact on the final product. This brings us back to the discussion of plot in Part I. Why does this fiction begin *at this moment?* What would happen if it began *here* instead? And does the plot move forward from the moment of its inception with ever-increasing tension, all the way to the climax?

Just as deleting a scene can make a huge difference in the impact of all that follows (and comes before), moving scenes around can up the ante for both your characters and your fiction. Once you truly understand how this powerful editing tool works, you'll be on the lookout for misplaced scenes as a matter of course.

I should note here that I (and my editor, bless her) have done this very thing with this chapter and the previous one. So this applies to nonfiction as well as fiction.

NOTE WHERE MY ATTENTION LAGS

Sometimes, I'll be reading and editing and then—*wham!*—dead stop. Suddenly, my mind wanders. What happened?

Because I'm alert to this occurrence, I make a note to consider deleting the entire scene and add a note that reads, "need a new scene here." Sometimes I realize exactly what the new scene needs to be as soon I write these words, and I'll make a few notes about that, as well. Sometimes a whole scene comes rushing out, and I scribble as fast as I can. (Usually I write in a circle around the page, then on the back, then on any other available surface. Yes, I know I ought to have a notebook handy for this, but for some reason, making a mess seems part of the process for me.) Sometimes no other scene is needed. And finally, sometimes—no, often—a scene can be picked up from somewhere else and inserted in place of the offending one.

IS IT AWKWARD?

You already know if something's awkward, because those intuitive alarms have been ringing like tinnitus. Sometimes, revising an awkward phrase makes it only more awkward still. This seems to happen, in particular, when we're trying to describe an action, such as, "Her elbows were on the table, and she put her chin in her hands."

So here are my suggestions for those awkward moments. First, consider whether you need the phrase at all. In the above example, you may be trying to show how she's feeling. But do you need to be quite so explicit about every aspect of her action? What if you simply said, "Chin in hands, she considered her options"?

Second, try rewriting the phrase from scratch rather than revising it to death. I like to do this with pen and ink rather than on the computer. If it's an entire paragraph that's awkward, so much the better. Don't look at what you've already written. You know what you want to say. Instead, try saying it again, differently.

IS IT THERE FOR THE WRITER OR FOR THE READER?

I know: You were hoping I wouldn't say this. You already know which passages I'm talking about, the ones that add nothing whatsoever to your fiction but which you simply can't bear to part with.

So listen: Don't part with them. Just put them in another file. Here's what I do in my computer: Each of my novels (each of my books, in fact, including this one) has its own directory. Each draft has a different name (usually, the month I began it). I also put all my Internet research material in this file, along with pictures, graphics, editorial guidelines, and other miscellany. In addition, there's a file called "Cuts." Every time I delete a section, long or short, from one of the drafts, I toss it in here. I don't pay any attention to order, although I do delineate between sections. I simply put this material away for another day, without getting rid of it entirely.

Here's the funny thing, though: I haven't gone back and used any of this discarded material yet. I think this is because I've been doing this a long time, and my instincts are usually right. But maybe, someday, I'll make something from all those discards. I also have a boardinghouse where characters I've deleted have moved. It's quite the place. Someday, I'll have to write a book about it.

QUESTIONS OF CHARACTER

Beyond the questions I've suggested above are a few that will help you consider how your characters act and interact. They're the ones driving your fiction, so if they go astray, the fiction could follow, and not always to the best ends.

With that in mind, here are two more questions to consider as you reread your manuscript. Both of them should help you get a handle on what to do with all those people hanging around in there.

ARE MY CHARACTERS TRUE TO THEMSELVES?

If everything you've set out about a character tells the reader she's shy and retiring, and then she suddenly walks into a room full of strangers and knocks 'em dead with her rendition of "My Heart Will Go On," your character's not being true to herself. Can the above scenario happen? Yes, it can. In fact, it can be the premise of your entire fiction: Wallflower learns to bring down the house.

But a shift like this must be earned. You can't simply insist a character is A and then suddenly have her doing B. If, in fact, she's doing B all the time, you need to get rid of the A stuff. In other words, if she constantly walks into rooms full of strangers and belts out Céline Dion's greatest hits, you likely need to lose all that stuff that suggests she's not that kind of gal.

IS MY DIALOGUE DOING ITS WORK?

While back in chapter seven, I talked at length about dialogue, this area of character development is one that very often needs some work during the revision stage. Why? First of all because, all too often, all of our characters end up sounding just like us. And, second, because we often either let them say too much or don't let them say enough.

Dialogue is the unsung hero of character development. Not only does it allow your characters to talk to each other, it can, succinctly and in just the right words, reveal how they feel about themselves, how they feel about each other, and how they feel about the world. Consider this exchange:

> "Harold? Are you listening to me?"
>
> "Hmm? What? Sorry, I wasn't listening."

I rest my case.

Pay Attention

As you do your Marathon Read-Through, keep in mind my going-to-the-bathroom test. Will your readers keep reading, even though they need to go the bathroom? Will they, finally, take your book to the bathroom with them? Or, will they suddenly find a place where they can stop and *put the book down?* You don't want this latter to happen. You want your readers to take the book with them. I gauge this by how *I* feel about what I'm reading: After all, if *my* attention lags while I'm reading my own book, it's pretty certain a reader's will, too.

You'll also want to be alert to those little nudges I mentioned at the beginning of this chapter, those intuitive signs that are telling you something isn't right. No matter how much you love a character, scene, paragraph, or word, whenever you get a nudge when you read it, either circle it or write yourself a quick note in the margin.

When I go back to the manuscript in my computer, I highlight these passages in a different color font or put brackets around them. Then I read the page, skipping over the passage. Ninety-nine times out of a hundred, the scene reads far better without the passage that I felt was somehow wrong. Even when I think I'm wrong, I'm right. That's what intuitive nudges are all about: saving us from ourselves.

After the Marathon Read-Through's Over

I like to put the whole project away for at least a week (again, preferably longer) after my Marathon Read-Through. This gives right brain time to mull some of the big-picture things I've learned about the fiction. I'm not, for the most part, consciously thinking about these issues, but I know my subconscious is subtly tossing and turning the new information and ideas.

When it's time (I know it's time because whatever right brain's been percolating shows up in left brain and starts nagging me), I copy the file, give it a new name (I use the month and year of the revision), and get to work. To begin, I park the marked-up manuscript next to my computer and begin going through it. This process is going to take me at least a month, sometimes a lot longer. In the next chapter, I'll show you why.

MINDING YOUR STORY
Coming Out of the Closet

You may not have a closet full of drafts, but you likely have any number of unfinished or unsatisfactory manuscripts that you abandoned at one time or another. What I'd like you to do is select one of these, ideally one you've not looked at for a number of years. A short story or chapter is ideal the first time you try this so you don't get overwhelmed or daunted by the task.

Select a time and place where you won't be interrupted and let those with whom you live know you won't answer pleas for anything short of abandoning a burning house. Arm yourself with a hard copy of your manuscript, pen or pencil (I like to gather several different color pens to denote different aspects), and your beverage of choice, and find a comfortable perch. Ready?

Read your manuscript. Note on the manuscript anything that pleases you or doesn't ring true. Your comments may run the gamut from "I still love this" to "What was I thinking?" with everything from "need more" to "cut this" in between. Be ruthless: This is editor-you, not creator-you. You may well decide not to heed your advice when you come back to it, but for now imagine that you are your own harshest critic.

When you're finished, consider what you've learned. Honestly, now, could you have been so critical if you'd started revision as soon as you had finished? Are you surprised by what time and narrative distance offer you in terms of critical power?

It's likely that next time, you'll be less surprised. And the time after that, you'll want to leave your manuscript in the closet for as long as you can.

chapter 17
PICKING UP THE PIECES

Did you know that Wolfgang Amadeus Mozart preferred to set a composition aside after completing a draft? Only months, or sometimes years, later would he pick it up, at which point he'd often rewrite sections over and over, even start entire movements from scratch. Mozart also tossed out far more than he ever published, because, yes, even Mozart wrote things with which he was less than satisfied.

What Mozart was doing was trying to make the music that others would ultimately hear match the music that was in his head. This process—making your final product match what's in your head—is what revision (whether of music, writing, or art) is all about. The tools in this chapter—creating a scene list; considering a change of tense, narrator, or even point of view; entering your changes into your computer; and starting (and using) your personal recycle bin—are all part of this process. Let's start with the scene list, the last big step before you begin the revision itself.

Creating a Scene List

When I'm ready for this phase of the revision process, I get out a new notebook. This is a great use for those gorgeous notebooks people are always buying me that I don't otherwise use, though I prefer the same kind of spiral notebook I used in high school and college, with a side binding and narrow-ruled pages.

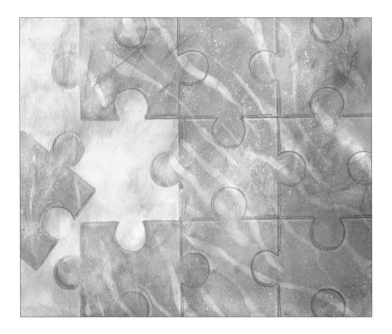

Once I've got notebook and pen ready, I sit down with my manuscript (I prefer to do this somewhere other than my desk, and still better, somewhere other than at home) and list each scene at the top of a new page. Using a new page for each scene is particularly important, as I'll be coming back to consider each one in a number of ways. I'm not reading the manuscript at this point, just noting each scene in the order in which it appears. Besides, because I've just finished my Marathon Read-Through, my manuscript is familiar enough that I know what each scene is about with a quick look at its opening lines.

I give each scene a heading, such as "A and her X fight in the hotel room in Athens." I keep these headings as brief, but as descriptive, as I can. Then, without writing anything else, I go on to the next scene (and a new page) and name it, as well, proceeding all the way through the fiction.

Once my scene list is finished, I go back through the list slowly and make notes about a number of things. What I'd like to do now is show you each of these individually, one step at a time.

SCENE-BY-SCENE QUESTIONS

The first set of questions concerns what I ask about each scene. I consider these four questions for each scene and only then go back and consider the last three, more holistic, questions.

1. DOES IT BELONG?

My first order of business is to determine how each scene fits into my bigger picture. If my fiction is about a woman who learns to trust herself, for example, it might begin with a scene that shows she doesn't trust herself and then move toward the moment when she realizes she can. That word "move" is key in any fiction. Each scene should in some way challenge my character while at the same time help move her toward that trust, or set her back.

My first scene, then, might be headed "*A* calls her *X* to ask his advice." Now, I'll note on the page what happens within the scene. Perhaps *X* tells *A* she needs to learn to trust herself, to rely on her instincts. *A* resists, *X* says he has to go and hangs up, and *A* is left back where she started, unsure of what to do.

Once I complete this synopsis, I answer the question, Does it belong? In this case, as this scene seems to set up the situation I invented above, I'll leave it as is, for now.

2. DOES IT BELONG WHERE IT IS?

Not only do I consider whether each scene belongs, but whether the order they're in best serves the story I'm trying to tell. What if, for example, I decided that the scene above is a terrific climactic scene, and I want to highlight the fact that *A can't* change? If that's the case, I have to re-examine what my fiction is about. If *A* can't change, after all, this fiction is not about a woman who learns to trust herself, but rather one who doesn't. This sort of what I call "stagnant fiction" (stagnant in that when its protagonist is faced with her ultimate challenge, she chooses not to change) can be compelling in the right hands, but it strikes me (at this particular moment) as a not very interesting way of presenting *A*'s story. So, in this case, the scene seems to belong where it is.

On the page in the notebook, I'll make a note of how the scene moves the story forward at the point where it currently is placed, as well as any other possible locations for it. I usually use a different color pen for this note.

3. IS IT FINISHED?

In my early short stories, whenever I got close to the heart of a conversation, a phone would ring. Then I'd insert a line break, and that would be that. Of course, my mentors were quick to point out that my fictions weren't doing what I wanted them to do because I wouldn't go where I feared to tread. Clearly, I wasn't digging deep enough.

Oh, I didn't want to go there! I'd had a lifetime of practice avoiding the places I didn't want to examine. But because I was (am) a fiction writer, those places were precisely the ones I most needed to not just enter, but examine, explore, and unravel.

And then, one night, I had a dream. (Really. It's true.) In the dream, I was climbing a ladder to the attic of my childhood home (only we had stairs, not a ladder, but you know how dreams are), carrying boxes of "stuff" up there for—for what? For safekeeping? To hide it?

Meanwhile, my brothers were shaking the ladder every time I climbed up with another box. I yelled at them to stop, but, of course, they're my younger brothers, and the more I hollered, the harder they shook. Suddenly, I realized I didn't need to carry these boxes up to the attic. I could use everything that was in them in my work.

At this revelation, I awoke. The dream was so vivid, I didn't even need to write it down. And its message was equally clear: Don't hide the "stuff" in boxes. Take it out and use it. Every last bit.

It's a tendency of beginning writers (and even many experienced ones) to end right at the climactic moment. You may object that each scene should end at a moment that keeps the reader wanting to read, but ending at the climax and leaving a question unanswered are not the same thing. In the latter case, your reader will keep reading because, despite the scene's resolution, something still remains unknown. Each scene will answer some questions but leave others unanswered—as well as pose a few new ones.

The key is to think of each scene in terms of rising action and ask if the scene completes itself. You already know whether your scene is finished, so even if you're resisting the possibility that it's not, your intuitive alarm will be the first to tell you otherwise.

If your scene isn't finished, write some notes about how it can be completed. Or finish it, right here, right now, in your scene-list notebook. If nothing occurs to me in the moment, I'll mark the page with a sticky tab (I adore sticky tabs!) so I finish the scene before I sit down to type in my edits.

4. DOES IT WORK?

Sometimes, alas, scenes simply have no place in the fiction at all. I've just started an entire novella from scratch after realizing that, while I had a great deal of fun writing scene after scene from a child's point of view, none of the scenes worked with the larger book of which the novella is a part. Try as I might, none of the scenes, characters, or lyrical descriptions could be saved, and last night I got out a new notebook and started the novella all over again.

As soon as I did this, by the way, the story took an unexpected turn. Now I can't wait to find out what happens next in my fiction. The lesson here is to admit when something doesn't work, because the thing that will work may be waiting to be discovered as soon as you sit down and start over.

In my scene list, I put one diagonal line across a scene I've decided to delete. That way, if I change my mind, I can still read my notes!

BIGGER-PICTURE QUESTIONS

Once you've looked at each scene individually, your next step is to consider the order of scenes from a big-picture perspective.

5. DO I NEED A SCENE THAT'S NOT YET HERE?

This question includes both the obvious—a central moment must be done in scene, not narrative—and those places where something inherent to a fiction's story arc is not yet on the page. My favorite example of this comes from an early novel of my own, in which one character repeatedly asks another to marry him throughout the course of the narrative, even though she is fatally ill. One of my readers suggested that it would be wonderful if, in the end, they did marry, even if the protagonist was in the hospital, on her deathbed. As soon as we hung up, I sat down and wrote a wonderful page-and-a-half wedding scene that, to me, remains the novel's crowning touch.

If your fiction needs scenes that aren't yet written, tear an empty page from the back of your notebook (or, if you can't stand to do this, use blank notebook paper) and insert it where the scene will go. Then make some notes about the new scene you're going to write, or, better still, write the scene itself. Very often, as in my example above, as soon as you know what's missing, the entire scene will spring whole from right brain.

6. WHICH QUESTIONS GET ANSWERED WHERE?

Remember those story-arc diagrams in chapter three? They will come in handy as you determine which questions are bigger than others. The biggest question will take the entire fiction to be asked and answered (or not answered, as Chekhov noted, but merely posed). Smaller questions may take place all in one chapter or even in one scene. Still others will be the stuff of your subplots, asked after and resolved before your biggest question.

In my scene-list notebook, I make a list of all the questions my fiction poses. Then I prioritize them, 1, 2, 3, etc. This leads naturally to the last scene-list question:

7. WHAT'S THE BIGGEST QUESTION IN YOUR FICTION?

This is the point when you need to reconsider which of your questions (see #2 and #6, above) is the biggest one of all. You may have initially written your fiction thinking it was about a woman who learns to trust herself, but now, as you go through your scene list, you realize that something that occurs all in one chapter—A's relationship with her X, say—is really the bigger question, the one on which you're interested in focusing.

Once you've established which question is the biggest, you can begin to reorder your scenes accordingly. You'll also go back to the beginning of *this* list of seven questions and look at each scene individually to determine if it still does all those things for your fiction.

CUT AND PASTE

At this point, I may actually take scissors to a copy of my manuscript and reorder it physically. It depends on how much moving around I've done. If I do create a new manuscript this way, I then reread it to see if it works for me. In this rereading, I look especially hard at transitions and flow, what works and what doesn't, tightening, nipping, and tucking.

Some writers generate a lengthy outline at this point (and I do mean lengthy; Jennifer Egan says hers run eighty pages; Mary Anna Evans's often run over one hundred). While I don't make an outline, the number of pages and length of time I spend working on my scene list amounts to almost the same thing. Your own method may be similar to mine or closer to Egan's or Evans's. The important thing is to find a way of working on revision that works for *you*.

IT AIN'T EASY

Revisiting your fiction this way is not just work—it's hard work. Still more important, it's a job for someone other than your creative self. That's why you've let your work sit in the closet for a while, so your sensitive side won't be hurt by all your pragmatic side's going to do at this stage.

Because the thing is, you've got to be merciless. You can't try to slip things by. You can't be lazy. You can't compromise, not ever. And you can't leave things for an editor to take care of. If you don't do this work now, you won't have that editor. Ever.

Ch-Ch-Ch-Changes

If, once you've completed your Marathon Read-Through and your scene list, something still feels off, it's time to consider what other changes might make a difference. Sometimes a simple change of point of view, from first to third person, for example, offers just the narrative distance you need to get your fiction back on track.

But sometimes a point-of-view change isn't enough. Sometimes you have to reconsider who's telling the story in the first place and whether your fiction shows to best effect with the narrator you currently have. The section I started over last night is being told from a different point of view, and, as I mentioned earlier, already is exciting to me all over again.

Finally, sometimes a fiction needs a change of tense. If this is the case, it won't simply be a matter of changing all the present tense verbs to past, or vice versa. That's because tense creates your fiction's mood as well, and as the mood changes with a tense change, so will the way you phrase certain things. Nonetheless, if you determine that this is what your fiction needs, it's worth the effort necessary to make it work. It can make all the difference.

Case Study

The novel I'm currently finishing has gone through more incarnations than the Dalai Lama. It began close to twenty years ago as a short story, morphed several years later into an entirely different short story, and then, at an MFA advisor's suggestion, was turned into a novel for the first time in 1993. It then went into that closet of mine for ten years. When it came out again, I tossed out quite a bit and wrote around much that was already there. The result was, in my agent's words, a mess.

She was right. Back in my closet it went, until this spring, when (for a number of reasons) the novel on which I'd been working lost its luster. This time, I began by deleting most of one character's sections, except for a frame at the beginning and end. Next I cut out everything that felt as if it didn't belong in the story I wanted to tell. By the time I was finished with all this slicing and dicing, I was left with about forty pages, a quantity approximately equal to the lengths of those two short stories with which I started twenty years ago.

WHAT DOES IT WANT TO BE?

Despite the lack of pages, I thought what I had was a novel, not a short story. I suppose I could have been daunted by the prospect of basically starting from scratch, but after so many years I was actually eager to revisit these characters and find out what they had to tell me now, what they'd withheld every other time I'd worked with them.

As someone who writes novels, short stories, poetry, reviews, essays, and nonfiction, I'm often asked how I know what any given piece of work is. To answer this question, I've come up with a checklist, although it's not something I actually use myself—I almost always "know" what something wants to be. Nonetheless it may be helpful for you as you consider what that idea knocking around your head wants to be.

+ A *short story* (unless it's by Alice Munro, which is a genre unto itself) shows a character in a state of flux. While other characters are present in a short story, it generally deals with one character's situation. Hence, short stories are almost always character driven.

+ A *novel* has a broader scope. Not only will it deal with a character's trajectory, there will be substrata and superstrata as well (at least if it's of the literary genre in which I write). You'll often find a number of leitmotifs, recurring ideas, or details that appear again and again. There may be a sustaining metaphor or ideas lingering just beneath the surface that are important, as well. A novel's larger idea (in high school, this was called the theme) is many-tentacled and won't always stay between the lines. Finally, a novel may be character driven or plot driven. With a few notable exceptions, most bestsellers fall into the latter category.

+ A *poem* moves between the small and the large. Poems may be concerned with language, an idea, a feeling or sense of something, or, really, just about anything, but without a fiction's overriding concern for character or plot. A good, complete poem will often leave the reader feeling as if something he's always known but been unable to articulate has for a moment been made clear.

+ Today's *literary nonfiction* and *essays* employ many of the tools of fiction, which has resulted in much better sales in this previously marginalized genre. Recent examples include Jon Krakauer's *Under the Banner of Heaven* and Sebastian Junger's *The Perfect Storm*. Literary (or narrative) nonfiction can be separated from literary fiction by the simple "it really happened" rule.

FROM MESS TO MEANING

Let's go back now to that forty pages with which I was left last summer. Why didn't I just start over, or see what of the hundreds of pages I'd cut might be used in some way? In effect, I *did* start over, because even the forty pages that were left required a great deal of rewriting and revision once I'd filled in the gaps between them. But even though the novel is still about the same thing, I approached the material in a new way that allowed me greater insight into my characters and their motivations. One of the things I realized shortly after I began, in fact, is that the novel would work far better if it were comprised of three stand-alone novellas that also worked together.

I wrote what I thought would be the last novella first, using some of the remaining material as my starting point. I spent some time fiddling with how the reordered material read, to get everything just so for what would come after, and then I wrote. And wrote. And wrote. By the time it felt right, it was November. I printed out what I had, scribbled all over it, and entered all the changes I'd made into a new document.

When I was finally ready to begin writing the other two novellas, I'd spent several months hanging around with these characters. They were who I dreamed about; they were who I thought about when I stared at the mountains out my window. I'd wake up in the morning suddenly, knowing something else that had happened to them that I hadn't known before. This is the stage where right brain is sending so much over to left brain that it's all I can do to keep up, and if you see me at this point, it's entirely possible I won't see you.

About a month later, I'd completed the second novella, the one I thought would be the first section. I printed it out, then got out my different colored pens and edited and added and subtracted; moved sections from one place to another; wrote notes to myself; and affixed sticky tabs where entire new scenes were needed. I began to see the shape of the thing. I could feel its direction and scope. I felt as if, this time, finally, I was getting it right.

STUCK IN THE MIDDLE

Then came the middle section. Comprised of entirely new material, it couldn't seem to get off to a good start. I tried everything—having my characters write letters, letting them rant at each other, even letting them rant at me.

The holidays came and went (and I came and went), but my novella was going nowhere. Then, my husband and I went on vacation, and I tried a few more false starts while we were gone. But nothing was working.

When we got back to the United States, though, a family crisis intervened, and, rather than head home, I had to fly up to Buffalo, where I'd grown up, to spend some time with my family. The events of that week, while hardly related to the novella I wrote when I got home (and yet, in a way, intimately related), provided precisely the seed I needed to write the middle section.

THE NEVER-ENDING STORY

And so, in late winter, I asked four of my first readers if they'd give what I had (70,000 words, by this time) a look. I gave two a list of specific issues I had with the novellas and told the other two nothing at all. (I'm nothing if not scientific.)

In the weeks that followed, I heard back from my readers, one at a time. In most ways, their comments were fairly consistent: All wanted more (or less) in the same places I knew I needed more (or less). All felt the characters were compelling, the story riveting, the basic idea clear and surprising. But (oh, that but!) three of them also felt that one of the novellas didn't work, and that, in addition, the order in which I'd put them was backward.

Meanwhile, while they were gone, I'd been reading my novellas again myself (always a sign there's more to be done). Something was off about the first section, I'd decided, though until I began the individual conversations with my readers, I couldn't pinpoint quite what. What's marvelous about readers you trust, though, is just how committed they become to your fiction. They'll brainstorm with you, play what-if, and talk about your characters as if they're real people, which, by this time, they truly seem to be. At the same time, the more you and a reader talk about your fiction, the more confident she will become about telling you what doesn't work, and why.

After these four conversations, I put the book away yet again. And then, last night, it burbled from my right brain to my left. "I'm ready," a narrator announced (and not the one who'd told that section most recently). So, I grabbed a notebook and a pen and began all over again.

I can't say enough times or enough different ways how important revision is in the writing process. For one thing, you might miss those moments such as I had when I was back in Buffalo. But, for another, if you send something out to an agent or editor before it's ready, it shows. And then you don't get another chance with that person. It's worth the effort to get it right so the first time's the charm, don't you think? I do.

Entering Your Changes Into Your Computer

As I have done time and again, I want to pause here to remind you that my methods may not end up being yours. I know that part of what I do is, quite simply, crazy, and here at the point when I start typing my edits into my computer is one of those moments. One reason I say this is because if I make a change in the file, I stop and scribble it onto my hard copy as well.

I think there are two reasons I do this (both of which suggest that perhaps there's a method to my madness after all). The first harkens back to over twenty years ago, when I worked for a software-development company whose reigning genius's preferred mode of working was to plop down in any employee's vacant seat and start typing code. The problem arose one day when I'd just completed a lengthy (over fifty pages and three months of work) piece of documentation for one of the company's products. I'd checked it, saved it, and (if you've worked in an office, you're familiar with this euphemism) gone down the hall.

When I got back to my desk, K. was sitting there, typing away. "Can I get in there a second?" I asked him. "I need to print out the manual I just finished." K. stood obligingly, but when I sat down, the manual was nowhere to be found. Nor could the mad software genius find it in the computer he'd commandeered. "Furious" is not a sufficient adjective for my feelings at that particular moment.

But even this disaster was a learning experience, because I learned the value of both backups and hard copies. So my first reason for recording whatever I type into the computer file onto the hard copy as well is backup, backup, backup.

My second reason is more visceral but, on reflection, no less valid. As I've said, I prefer to do my editing longhand, so when I record an edit on the manuscript after I've typed it, I also get a sense of whether it feels right. It's easy to type edits (especially when you type as fast as I do), but it's equally easy to lose the feeling of the words when you do. Hence, this double duty is a way of checking my work in order to make sure it looks, feels, and sounds the way I mean it to.

TYPING IN MY EDITS

Ultimately, this phase of revision/rewriting is for me a secretarial chore. I've already done the hard work of editing and am now simply typing in what I've done. But both because I type fast and because I'm dyslexic, what I type in is often hysterically funny (or worse, obscene: Look at the letter below "r" on your keyboard and you'll see how I've mistyped the word "truck" more than once). That's why, after each new insertion (long or short), I stop and read what I've typed, aloud. Why aloud? Because that's the only way to slow me down enough to catch these dumb mistakes.

But typing in my edits also involves moving chunks of material. What I do to help me with this is use letter designations and page numbers on my manuscript that denote what will be moved where (see appendix B for a sample page from one of my edited manuscripts). I'll write "move to A, pg. 33" next to the section, and "insert A from 15" in the new location. Also, I don't simply cut and paste; I copy and paste and then go back and cut so I'll be able to keep the page numbering straight when I go to the new location. (And also because of the lesson from above: backup, backup, backup.)

CHAPTER 17

Starting (and Using) Your Personal Recycle Bin

Of course, the other thing that happens when I'm typing in my edits is that I cut out swaths of material, sometimes mere paragraphs, but often pages and pages. I'm referring here to material that's not being moved, as above, but that I'm not going to use in this manuscript at all.

Throw it out? you're thinking. Talk about a gut-clenching prospect. I really *do* recommend tossing the trash, but if you can't bear to part with a word (and there are plenty of words I can't stand to lose completely), set up a separate file. This can be on your computer or in an actual folder or notebook. I have files set up for each novel's deletions. Some (no, most) of them are longer than the novels themselves. And, of course, there's that boardinghouse, where all the characters I've cut still reside, just waiting for their own moments to be sent over from right brain.

But the main reason your gut clenches at the prospect of major cutting is that it takes guts to know when your beloved prose simply isn't working. That's why, even though for the past few weeks I'd been trying to save what I could from that seventy-page novella that wasn't working, I ultimately decided, once and for all, that the book wasn't going to work until I, yet again, started that section over and rewrote it. So much of this is gut instinct that I want to, once more, stress those intuitive nudges.

The other thing I've learned about such occasions is that I can't force something to be written until it's ready. At least three of my novels (including the current manuscript) and many more of my short stories ultimately succeeded because I had the good sense to leave them be until something happened in my life that provided the missing seed. So trust yourself, and trust the ways of the world. While trying to finish a fiction before it's ready to be finished is an exercise in futility, finishing it when it *is* ready is one of the great joys of the writing life.

MINDING YOUR STORY
Scene List Checklist

I covered a lot of ground in this chapter, so much that you may have been considering creating a crib sheet. Well, good news! I've created one for you. Here, one by one, are the steps for creating your scene list.

Scene-By-Scene Questions

1. Does it belong?
2. Does it belong where it is?
3. Is it finished?
4. Does it work?

Bigger-Picture Questions

5. Do I need a scene that's not yet here?
6. Which questions get answered where?
7. What's the biggest question in your fiction?

chapter 18
OTHER READERS, OTHER ROOMS

Chances are, you fantasized about your book on the front-of-store display of your local mega-bookstore long before you got up the nerve to show it to one person, maybe even before you wrote a word. That's because while most writers have no problem imagining masses of strangers reading their work, the possibility of those who know them best reading it scares them so much many never begin writing at all.

But whether you choose to have individual readers, belong to a formal critique group, or attend writers workshops, classes, or seminars, getting feedback from readers other than yourself is one of the most important things you'll do as you begin to revise and rewrite your fiction. In this chapter, I'll look in depth at what you can expect from each of these methods toward revision, and show you how you can make the most of your outside readers, whether they're writers like you or "mere" family and friends.

Revision by Committee

Revision means, literally, "re-seeing" something you've looked at before. In Great Britain, in fact, "revision" means to review material and includes studying for examinations. I like this way of thinking about the process of revision and encourage you to incorporate it into your lexicon, even if you're on this side of the Great Pond.

If your first outside readers are your friends and family, chances are they will say something like, "Wow! This is great! You should publish it." That's all well and good, but it's not the kind of constructive criticism you need at this point. You need readers who will both take an active interest in your fiction and understand how fiction works. A good reader will be able to tell you not just that something's off about a character but that the character didn't seem true to himself because of something specific, here on page 27, or that they wish you had a scene where Q happens between W and Y.

That's why the different point of view offered by outside readers is a great revision tool. Not only will critiquers discover your typos and inadvertently omitted words, they'll have expectations for your manuscript that it may not have yet fulfilled. The best outside readers will be able to articulate not just what those expectations are, but suggestions for how you can move from your current draft to a manuscript that fulfills their—and your—expectations.

WHOM SHOULD YOUR OUTSIDE READERS BE?

The first question you'll need to address about outside readers is whom you should ask to read your manuscript in the first place. While it may be tempting to go straight to editors and agents, unless you're a seasoned self-editor, this is almost always a big mistake. Not only will you have missed those typos and word omissions, but your fiction may well be missing that *je ne sais quois* that will separate it from the pack.

Outside readers can help you figure out what's missing, but it's important to select the *right* ones. Other writers are a good choice because they're familiar with the process, but I like to use nonwriter readers, as well, because they bring such a different sensibility to the process. The most important thing about your outside readers, though, is that they be readers whose judgment you trust and from whom you'll be comfortable receiving constructive criticism without arguing about every word and idea.

Other Writers

There are other writers, and then there are other writers. My current group of outside readers includes a playwright, an editor, a novelist, and a writing teacher. Two of these women have never been published (though they deserve to be). Each of them brings a very different sensibility to the table.

One of my outside readers is a marvel when it comes to moving things around on the page, whether it's words, sentences, or larger chunks of material. Another is much stronger on story than I am, and still another is, like me, a big-picture reader. One of my favorite readers is a friend who's a professional editor. Because she doesn't pull any punches, I've closeted more than one novel indefinitely based on her thoughts.

When you give your outside readers your manuscript, you can either ask for feedback about specifics or simply give them the manuscript and ask for their reaction. Always bear in mind, however, that this is a very big thing you're asking of them, and you'll want to do the same for them whenever you can. I'm sorry to say that I once fell prey to a (former) friend who asked me to read and comment on her first novel many, many times, only to claim she "wasn't interested in that kind of stuff" when I asked her to read one of mine.

The best thing about having other writers critique your work is that, if they're good, you'll soon incorporate their voices into your head as you write. "I'd better take a moment to say what this character looks like, for Arnold," you'll say, or, "Mabel won't like if I use the vague term 'something' here." Then you'll come up with something (sorry, Mabel—couldn't resist!) far better.

Writers' Groups

While I've been in only a few writers' groups myself, I've led many more, and I have to say that groups with a leader often work far more effectively than the more cooperative kind. But this depends a lot on the personalities involved. Sometimes the loudest voice is the weakest critic (and often, the weakest writer), while the quiet person, who doesn't speak unless spoken to, will offer the criticism you'll value most.

The best thing you can do when your writers' group is just starting out is set up some rules. If you're in a book group, you already know that the better the rules, the better the group functions, and the same is true of a writers' group. Your rules should ideally include: how many pages each writer is expected to share each time (minimum and maximum); whether you want to send pages in advance or read aloud at meetings; whether each writer is required to submit pages each time or members will rotate manuscript submissions; the number of members; whether the person whose work is being critiqued can speak while others are talking about his work (more about the Code of Silence when I talk about more formal workshops and classes, later in this chapter); how often you'll meet; and time and timing issues.

FINDING A CRITIQUE GROUP

If you find it difficult to look at your own work critically, finding a writers' group whose members understand the value of constructive criticism will help you learn how to do so. Some groups are led by a more experienced writer (I currently meet with several groups of former students three or four times a year); others are made up of peers. Always start with the big stuff (character, plot, pacing) and move to the small stuff (grammar, word choice, spelling) only if there's time (if at all). It's all too easy for a group to lose the proverbial forest for the trees, so make sure at the outset that your critique group has a commitment to the big picture.

You can find a critique group in a number of ways. If there's a local college or university nearby, check their bulletin boards (or the bulletin boards of one of the coffee shops near it). Better yet, if there's a local writers' organization, go to a meeting and see what it's about. Because everyone there was once in the same position you are now and will remember how hard it was to take that first step through the door, you'll likely get a warm welcome.

If, like me, you live in a rural area or small community, there are still plenty of options. Many librarians know who's writing and will direct you to others interested in starting critique groups. There's also the Internet. Finding a writers' group via a Web search that includes the words "writing group" and the name of your town is amazingly simple. I just Googled "writing group Corrales NM" (my small village of nine thousand people), for example, and got 38,100 hits! Finally, quite a number of my former students love the online groups they've found through writers' sites like www.writersdigest.com and www.authorlink.com.

The hardest step in joining a critique group is the first one. But trust me: If it's the right group, these people will become some of the best friends you'll ever have.

GETTING THE MOST FROM A CRITIQUE GROUP

I firmly believe that you will get far more from critiquing others' works-in-progress than from the critiques you receive of your own work. Why? Because it's in discovering what's wrong with someone else's manuscript that you will learn how to discover what's wrong with your own.

That said, many writers' groups are dysfunctional. I think it's the nature of writers themselves that makes this so: The best writers are generally introverts (including, hard as it may be for you to believe at this point, me) and so are hesitant to stop writers' group bullies, long-winded critiquers, and other problem characters. To help you head these characters off at the pass, though, I've developed this quick guide to some of the more egregious offenders.

IN CHICAGO, WE ...

In Chicago always knows better than everyone else, because when she lived there (such a far better place than here that you wonder why she ever moved here), they did things this way. Of course, it doesn't have to be Chicago. It can be Santa Fe or Cincinnati or even Scotia, Nebraska (I once lived there; the population was 250 and going down fast). The problem with In Chicago is that she won't listen to anyone else's way of doing things and, in addition, often dominates dialogue with tangents that offer no helpful critique.

There are a number of ways to curtail In Chicago. One is a firm rule that only the work at hand be discussed. If such a rule isn't in place, this is one of those moments when a workshop leader comes in handy, someone who can say, "Let's stick to the topic, please" without In Chicago getting so far bent out of shape, she's in Indiana.

MARIAN, MADAME GRAMMARIAN

One of my hard-and-fast workshop rules is that critique time not be spent on little things like spelling and grammar. Yes, grammar's important—*very* important—but what's more important to discuss in a critique group is the bigger picture. If a manuscript's grammar is so bad the problem stands in the way of reading it, then suggest the offender buy, read, and read again, Strunk and White's *The Elements of Style*.

Nonetheless, there will almost always be someone in the group who feels it his duty to point out every misuse of pluperfect and the wrong "discrete" (I've got that page tabbed in my dictionary, as I can't keep them straight myself). To my mind, critique-group time is far better spent talking about fiction, not grammar, hence the "Start with the big stuff" rule.

If Marian, Madame Grammarian insists on being heard, suggest that she line edit the manuscript and discuss it with the offender afterwards. Chances are, she'll do this anyway, but this way, valuable group time won't be taken up learning how to diagram sentences.

MISTER KNOW-IT-ALL

Like In Chicago, Mr. Know-It-All has been there, done that. Quick to interrupt and slow to give up the floor once he has it, Mr. KIA has an answer for every problem he perceives in any manuscript not his own. The problem is, he's not always right. In fact, he's often wrong. Worse still, he often strays from the topic at hand to something that's of far more interest to *him*.

Mr. KIA can be curtailed by setting out rules for how a manuscript is discussed in the first place. When discussing a manuscript's plot, critiquers might cite a plot from a published book to make their points, for example. But if such rules aren't in place, someone else will have to keep Mr. KIA to task. You, maybe?

MISS PRISS

Miss Priss is Mr. KIA's opposite: She'll never volunteer a thing, never interrupt, and, when she does speak, she will begin by saying that she may be wrong. The thing is, Miss Priss is often the most insightful critiquer in the group.

In a previous incarnation of my current writers' group, whenever one of the women read one of her poems, another woman always began her critiques by saying, "I don't know anything about poetry, but ..." and then proceeded to offer the perfect piece of criticism to bring the poem to the next level. So one morning after the poet read, when it was Miss Priss's turn, I turned to her and said, "I don't know nuthin' 'bout poetry," a reference (for those few mortals who haven't read *Gone With the Wind*) to Scarlett O'Hara's slave, Prissy, who "don't know nuthin' 'bout birthin' babies."

As Miss Priss is originally from North Carolina, the line got a laugh. But it further alerted everyone—especially Miss Priss—that she did, after all, know a great deal about poetry.

Humor is a great way to acknowledge the contributions Miss Priss can make to your group. But so is respect for whoever is speaking. If you're in a group full of interrupters (as I am), you must make a rule that when Miss Priss speaks, everyone listens.

IN MY MANUSCRIPT ...

It's tempting at this point for me to offer one of those dichotomies for which I'm famous in my own little world: There are two kinds of writers, the self-effacing and the self-promoting. In My Manuscript, an example of the latter kind, simply can't keep to the task at hand. No matter whose manuscript is being discussed, he commandeers the conversation and turns it back to his own work.

Not only is this unfair to the person whose work is being critiqued, it's disrespectful to all the writers in the group. When IMM invokes his favorite pronoun, it's immature and immaterial. Discussion should be limited to the manuscript at hand. Add that to your list of rules and smoke it.

THE CODE OF SILENCE

All right, I've mentioned it twice. It's time to address what the Code of Silence is all about. The problem with allowing the person who's being critiqued to talk is that so much of what we hear feels as if it needs rebutting. The Code of Silence keeps us from doing this, which is a good thing. Here's why.

First of all, it doesn't matter to a fiction if "it really happened." The action in a fiction furthers its plot. If something doesn't move it forward, it doesn't belong there.

Second, your readers have taken the time to consider and comment on your manuscript, and in return, you owe them the respect of listening to their thoughts without argument.

Third, and most important, no matter how much you may think you disagree with someone's initial assessment, chances are, on reflection, you'll begin to see that what she's suggesting is precisely what your manuscript needs. If you keep interrupting, however, you may well miss these important cues.

The only exception to the Code of Silence is to answer a direct question from one of the other participants, such as, "Will we find out later who D is?" or "Is this a rewrite of the chapter we read a few months ago?" In the writing groups I lead, I insist that direct questions be answered yes or no, without elaboration. I'm also the one who graces transgressors with a tilt of the head and a smile, which is enough to remind them the Code of Silence is in effect.

Writing Conferences, Workshops, Seminars, Classes, and MFA Programs

Boy, did I manage to group a lot of different things under one header! But it's intentional, because all of these various venues offer basically the same thing: professional writers leading workshops, contact with editors and agents, critique groups with writers just like you (and sometimes led by published authors), learning environments, the opportunity to meet and befriend writers whose careers (or lack thereof) are at the same point as yours, and, in the last case (with apologies to Dr. Science), the possibility to get an MFA—in writing!

There are as many kinds of conferences, workshops, seminars, classes, and MFA programs as there are writers. Some are focused on marketing. Many are genre-oriented. Some last a day, some a week, some a semester or longer. The question is, what do *you* want from one of these options? Here are some considerations for you:

1. If you're just starting out, a writers conference in your vicinity (as opposed to one farther away) will allow you meet others just like you, as well as get a feel for how such things work in the first place. In Albuquerque, for example, there's a group called SouthWest Writers that offers biweekly meetings with a speaker, quarterly daylong seminars that focus on a specific genre, a critique service, plus a nationally respected writing contest. In central Florida, there's a wonderful group called Writing the Region that sponsors the Marjorie Kinnan Rawlings Writing Conference each summer, and which includes a tour of Cross Creek, Rawlings's home. In addition, both coasts of the United States (as well as the heartland) are teeming with possibilities. I teach at the Santa Barbara Writers Conference each year, so of course recommend it especially highly!

2. If you've been writing for a while, consider attending a workshop, seminar, or class that covers a topic with which you've been having difficulty. My approach to this was to scour a conference's listings for the names of writers whose work I loved, and then ascertain if they were offering classes or workshops that would address my problem area. But you should also make it a habit to download conference programs for details on the classes being offered, and ask questions of writers or organizations offering classes. And don't be afraid to ask questions when you're in a class. I can't tell you how many times I've given a class, asked if there were questions and

gotten no response, then had all twenty students come up to me afterward asking precisely the same question. There are no stupid questions, only unasked ones.

3. What can you afford? If you're strapped for money, stick close to home. There are plenty of good options besides the Maui Writers Conference (see #1, above).

4. Most important, what are your expectations? Do you want to work one-on-one? Do you want to have an agent or editor session? Do you want to simply sit and listen to talks and presentations? Do you want to meet other writers, both published and unpublished, in a comfortable setting? Do you want to teach writing? (To me, that's the primary reason to pursue an MFA in writing.) Make a list of what you want from anything writing-related you might attend, and then steer your plans to your desires.

Critique Services

How do you find someone to edit and/or critique your work outside of the above options? My first suggestion is to try doing an Internet search for critique services in your area. But if that search doesn't turn up anyone in whom you have confidence, there are other options. You can, to name but a few, contact local writers' organizations and ask them, read the listings in writing magazines like *Writer's Digest* and *Poets & Writers*, ask other writers for referrals, or approach a writer you've met through a class or even a signing (you'd be surprised how many of us also offer critiquing, for a fee).

Because I only critique work that has already been highly polished (except when I'm teaching, of course), I charge a high hourly rate and accept very few manuscripts. But I also refer people to a number of other editors, based on what I believe the author's needs and level of experience are. One of the editors to whom I refer work is a wonderful copy editor. Another is very good at seeing the big picture. Still another loves working so closely with an author that the resulting manuscript ends up being more a collaborative than an individual effort.

So if there's a writer you think you'd like to approach to critique your work, all it costs you is the question. Even if he says no, he may well give you a referral such as I do.

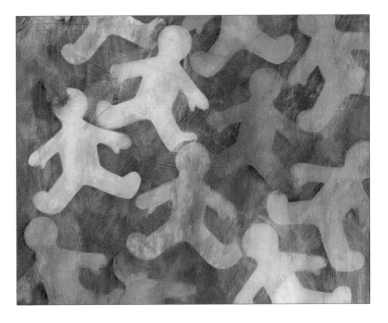

Readers as Readers

Astute readers are fabulous critiquers, without the competitiveness that occasionally (even though it shouldn't) creeps into a writer-to-writer critique. If you do ask readers to critique a manuscript-in-progress, how-ever, make clear to them that you're looking for specifics for improving the manuscript, not glory and praise. While other writers, and of course editors, agents, and writing teachers, will know how to critique, you may need to show this chapter to a reader/critiquer so he'll understand how the game is played.

But whether it's a writers' group, conference, class, seminar, or reader, whom you choose to critique your precious manuscript ultimately will be up to you. Just make sure your readers are people who care as much about it being all it can be as you do. Then, sit back and reap the benefits.

MINDING YOUR STORY
The Seven Commandments of Critiquing

There are as many ways to organize a critique group as there are critique groups. Because I lead several regular writing workshops, however, I've found it helpful to come up with some rules and regulations by which my students (and their writing) live and die. And so here are the Seven Commandments of Critiquing (only God could come up with ten):

1. Thou shalt remain silent when thy work is being discussed. The exception is to directly respond—briefly—to someone's question.

2. Thou shalt treat all manuscripts as thou would wish to have thine own treated, with respect and reverence for the work that has already gone into them.

3. Thy comments shall be constructive rather than merely critical. Rather than, "This doesn't work for me," for example, thou shalt say, "This doesn't work for me because ___ ."

4. Thou shalt stick with the big stuff: concept, character, plot, and pacing.

5. Thou shalt note the small stuff (grammar, spelling, etc.) on the manuscript rather than take up workshop time with it—unless it speaks to larger issues.

6. Thou shalt not, during another's workshop, talk about thyself or thine own work. Thou shalt confine thy comments to the work at hand.

7. Thou shalt remember that thy will learn as much, if not more, from critiquing someone else's work-in-progress as from having thine own work critiqued.

chapter 19
THE BIG PICTURE

Between your own Marathon Read-Throughs and the input from your outside readers, by now you may have accumulated hundreds, if not thousands, of pages with notes on your fiction. Your task now that the critiques are over is to consider what you have to do in order to begin putting your manuscript together again. (And yes, the Humpty Dumpty allusion is intentional.)

For me, this rethinking and reassembly process is the most rewarding aspect of writing a fiction. This is the time when I compare what I have with what I want and consider the chasms between them, nipping and tucking my manuscript into its final form. In order to do this, though, I first must ascertain the big picture—what my fiction's about.

What's It About?

How many words does it take you to answer this question? You should be able to sum up your book in one telling sentence, and if you can't do this easily, it likely means your novel still needs work. How can I say this with such authority? Because until I could come up with such a sentence for each of my novels, something was still missing. Now I can tell you that *Dissonance* is about a mysterious legacy that sends a Los Alamos piano teacher on a journey of self-discovery, and that *Coyote Morning* is about two women in a New Mexico village who learn that life's greatest threats arise far more often from those you already know than from those you don't.

ONE SENTENCE, ONE SIMPLE SENTENCE

Those two sentences of my own notwithstanding, I'm continually amazed when I read one-sentence descriptions of fictions. In the commercial genre, of course, it's easy to come up with one sentence: "When a mad entrepreneur uses DNA to bring dinosaurs back to life for his theme park, all hell breaks lose." But in the literary genre, it's often harder to boil all your ideas down into one simple sentence.

One difficulty is that, in a literary novel, what appears to be at stake on the surface and what's really at stake are often two different things. This is why I've come up with a formula for answering the question, "What's it about?"

protagonist + what's at stake = what it's about

How does this work? Let's look at two recent literary bestsellers by way of example. In Mark Haddon's *The Curious Incident of the Dog in the Night-Time*, while the autistic young narrator focuses on the death of a neighbor's dog, what's really at stake is his own carefully constructed world. Similarly, in Yann Martel's *Life of Pi*, the narrator focuses on day-to-day survival when what's really at stake is the very nature of reality and the way we remember what happens—or doesn't happen.

This may sound deceptively simple, but when you try to apply it to your own fiction, you'll see that it's not. I can easily write "about statements" for others' works-in-progress, but that doesn't mean the concept is on the page; it just means I've gotten good at figuring out what someone's trying to say, even if he hasn't said it yet. For example, I can tell that the novel one of my students is working on is about a man looking back at his life—but it isn't yet about the larger issue she'd like it to be. Nor is the novel another student is rewriting about a young woman who learns that people are not what they seem. The reason neither of these descriptions sounds distinctive enough is that the novels don't yet show what's at stake on the page.

Again, I must reiterate that I have a hell of a time with this when it comes to my own novels. I'd like to say that part of the problem is that I almost always have more than one narrator, but having recently read Ann Cummins's multiple-point-of-view *Yellowcake*, which is about how the latent dangers of uranium mining affect the lives of several families living in a Four Corners community, it's clear that's not a legitimate excuse.

With that in mind, I'll use my formula, take a leap, and say that the novel on which I'm still toiling away (concurrently with writing this book) is about how a woman's difficulties with (no, not difficulties with … disagreements with? dislike for? distrust of?) her stepdaughter years before reverberate for not only her own daughter, but her granddaughter, as well.

The fact that I'm still quibbling with myself about the wording tells me I've still got work to do, but, using the formula above, it's also clear to me I'm getting closer. Protagonist ("a woman") + what's at stake ("distrust of her stepdaughter") = what it's about ("reverberations in future generations"). Notice, too, that active verb, "reverberate." I would argue that in order to write a good summary sentence about a literary novel, you've got to know what your primary active verb is.

Why don't you try the same thing for your own novel and see if you can easily answer the question of what it's about by determining what your primary active verb is? If despite all these guidelines you still come up short, you've got more work to do.

From Big Idea to Scenes That Work

Once you know what's at stake for your protagonist, you're ready to look at what you have and see how it fits into this larger picture. At this point, it's likely you've read your fiction at least fifty times (especially its earlier sections, which of course get read more than the later ones because they've been around longer). Plus, you've probably printed out hard copies at least ten different times, marked each up, and then typed your edits into files saved with different names.

When I get to this step in the revision process, I select one of the copies of the manuscript I've gotten back from a reader. I usually select the one with the notes that mirror my own thoughts most closely. With that copy next to my computer (I've got this great acrylic recipe holder that I stand the manuscript in so I can see it without compromising my posture), I open the most recent file and then immediately save it with a new name (April 2008 rewrite.doc, for example). Then I get to work.

YOU, THE TYPIST

At this stage, rather than read through the fiction yet again, I'm going to go straight to each note on the manuscript and edit (or not edit) the new file in my computer based on that note. If the reader has asked for a new scene, I'll switch to a red or blue font and type {new scene here}, and if the new scene arises full-blown at that moment, I'll type it in as well (although I prefer to do this after this step, in a separate file; see below). If there's been a suggestion for a cut or move, I'll copy and then paste the longer sections before deleting them from their current locations. I'll pick up and drag shorter sections, although you should be very careful when you do this, especially if you're dyslexic like me. I've found dragged sections in wrong spots more than once when I've gone back to read the manuscript again, and while the mistaken placements are sometimes laugh-out-loud funny, more often they make no sense whatsoever, and I can't always figure out where they belong.

After I get through this first reader's copy, I go back to the beginning and start all over with my next reader's notes. I've found that not only is it far easier to enter my edits this way than to have five copies spread across my desk (even though I have this lovely, large library table my husband built for me years ago), but with each pass-through, I often see other areas that could stand improvement as well.

FILLING IN THE BLANKS

After I've gone through each of my readers' marked-up manuscripts, I read and consider any additional notes they've given me. (I prefer on-manuscript notes, but some readers like to write—and some writers like to read—additional thoughts.) Whenever I come across something worth considering, I either mark it with a highlighter or red pen or rewrite it on my own scribble sheet. (There is—horrors!—a sample of one of my scribble sheets in appendix C.)

By the time I finish this task, it's the next day, or the day after that, and chances are I've been subconsciously considering my new scenes while performing the mostly left-brain task of entering all those edits. Now it's time to write the missing scenes.

I create a new file for each new scene. That way, if it doesn't work, I don't have to yank it back out of my main manuscript file. But if it does work (and usually, now that I do it this way, it will), I can pick it up and move it over with just a few keystrokes and also have it saved on its own, just in case. (Backup, backup, backup.) I do, as I recently found out, have to be careful to delete any material the new scene replaces.

The next morning, I print out each new scene and read it over, marking it up and then entering my edits, just as I do for the whole fiction. I usually have to print it out and mark it up at least twice, and often three times, before I move the scene into the main file.

I should note that the same is true for chapters of this book, my columns for Authorlink.com, book reviews, short stories—in fact, everything I write. I print out a draft, scribble all over it, type in my edits, print out a new copy, scribble all over that, and print it out again. I use both sides of a piece of paper when I print, so this isn't quite the waste of paper it sounds. I also hang on to the particularly messy drafts because I love to show my students what I mess a make.

It's also worth noting that I edited my work this way, marking up hard copies, even when I wrote my drafts longhand and used an IBM Selectric typewriter. Being able to save everything in a computer file has made the process easier, but it hasn't changed the way I write and rewrite very much at all.

MARKING IT UP, AGAIN

Once you've written, edited, and moved all your new scenes into the main file, it's time, again, for yet another Marathon Read-Through. This Marathon Read-Through is going to be a little different, though. I sit down with my scene-list notebook and once again make a page for each scene. I note who's in each scene, when on the novel's timeline it occurs (because my fictions don't always proceed chronologically, this is particularly important), what happens in the scene, what changes occur from the beginning to the end of the scene, and, most important, what purpose the scene serves in the larger novel.

It's possible that at this point I'll decide that one or two scenes still need a bit more, or even that there are places where another scene is needed. But I should be getting close. I can feel it, when I'm almost there.

If, for any reason, you find you keep putting off this task, you need to ask yourself why you've lost interest in your fiction, because no matter how many times you read a fiction of your own, it should continue not only to hold your interest but also to have you thinking about it in new ways. Remember, if your fiction can't keep *your* attention, it's unlikely to keep anyone else's.

"BE VIOLENT AND ORIGINAL"

As I'm sure is clear by now, I have a great deal of respect for the mayhem that ultimately leads to a manuscript of which I'm proud. Taped to my printer is this quote from Gustave Flaubert: "Be regular and orderly in your life ... so that you may be violent and original in your work," to remind me that I can afford to be messy in my early drafts because the more I revise, the more meticulous I'll become about fitting all the pieces together.

And yes, my house is quite tidy and orderly. But that said, I have writer friends whose houses are disaster areas, and guess what? They're far more organized in their writing. Which just goes to show you: We each have our own way of working. Always remember that you don't need to mimic what I do precisely. So long as you keep working, ultimately, you'll come to your own methods—and madnesses.

For me, the process of fine-tuning a novel is like finishing a weaving. Every thread, every color, every pattern is part of the whole. I check to see that every thread is pulled tight, that none are left hanging. I test the weaving for strength and see how it looks in different lights. Only when I'm satisfied with it from every angle do I let it go out into the world.

How Do I Know When It's Finished?

Listen: You'll never be thoroughly satisfied with your fiction. Even when (note I didn't say "if") it's published, you'll find things you wish you'd said or done differently. That said, there is a very certain "yes" moment when you know you've done all you can and it's time to send your fiction out into the world.

I like to illustrate my answer to this question with a story about a story. A few years ago, I got some old short stories out of the closet (yes, that same closet). I read each one, pen in hand, and found that some (including some of those published) were dreadful. Others, though, were intriguing. They weren't, to my mind, remotely ready to send out. But something about them recaptured my interest, and I began to rewrite them, one at a time. And I do mean "rewrite": Often the new stories' only commonality with the old was the title or a line or two.

When the first of those retooled stories was ready, I considered something I hadn't in years—sending it to an editor "over the transom" (another synonymous phrase for unsolicited submissions you'll often hear is "from the slush pile"). I have connections with a number of editors now, but that wasn't what I wanted. I wanted validation from someone who'd never heard of me or my work. I set my bar high because I had a great deal of confidence in that story and sent it to a literary magazine for which I've long had a great deal of respect. A part of me knew I was setting myself up for disappointment, but after ten years of not sending out stories, I felt I could shoulder the risk. To my surprise and joy, *The Southwest Review* bought that story.

So my final word to you on this subject is that the work is worth it. Truly. It is.

MINDING YOUR STORY
What's It About?

Try using the formula I mentioned at the beginning of this chapter to answer this question about one of your own fictions in one sentence.

protagonist + what's at stake = what it's about

Keep in mind that an active verb that links your protagonist to what's at stake is key here.

If you can't yet answer the question, "What's It About?" in one sentence, you've still got work to do. But keep up the good work! You're almost there.

chapter 20
SELF-CONFIDENCE AND THE WRITING LIFE

One of your most important tools as a writer is the ability to keep your senses open to everything around you—not simply seeing but listening, smelling, tasting, touching, and, most difficult of all, being open and empathetic to everyone (and everything) with whom you come in contact. Being this sensitive isn't easy, which is why, I suspect, so many of us must regularly retreat into our hidey-holes to recover from our forays into the outside world. In fact, I'm sure (if anyone has studied such a thing) that most writers must be Is—introverts, people who find their restorative moments occur when they're alone—on the Myers-Briggs scale.

It's all the more ironic, then, that we open, receptive, caring, oversensitive sorts must learn to shoulder rejection far more often than other mere mortals. No, not just shoulder it, but accept it and then as quickly as possible expose the rejected part of ourselves yet again, long before the hurt has begun to heal. How such a receptive creature can at the same time develop a thick skin is perhaps the greatest paradox of the writing life. The truth is, we don't. With each rejection comes that all-too-familiar sinking feeling, the one we'll carry around all that day—and sometimes, far longer.

So how do we do it? In this last chapter of *The Mind of Your Story*, I'd like to share some of my thoughts about this most difficult aspect of the writing life.

The Thicker the Skin, the Harder the Fall

On the one hand, we writers have to be far more self-assured than those who work in fields with regular assessments, or even those who work with others who remind them of their worth. Most writers (to paraphrase Thoreau) live lives of quiet desperation, working mostly on our own until we send something out into the larger world, only to (far too often) get a preprinted piece of paper back a few months later, telling us our labor of love is not what that world is looking for.

And yet, what do we do? We send it out again. And again. The percentages against us are staggering. Even a small literary magazine, one with, say, a circulation of five hundred, will accept only a small number of the manuscripts it receives. And a well-known venue like *The New Yorker* publishes something received over the transom so seldom that the event makes publishing headlines for its very rarity.

Few writing books deal with this fact of the writing life, yet it's so intrinsic to it that I don't feel I can conclude this book without discussing it. First, though, I'd like to suggest that you increase your odds of success by doing precisely what I've suggested throughout this book: Polish your manuscript until you know it's everything it can be.

UNFINISHED BUSINESS

Nearly all overworked editors (and really, there is no other kind) will tell you that ninety percent (or more) of the unsolicited manuscripts they receive should never have left the post office in the first place. Among the more obvious errors editors cite are everything from improper formatting (a recent Internet search on this topic netted over a million hits), to poor spelling and grammar, to material simply not suited for the publication to which it was submitted (this, my editor notes, is the most common mistake).

So Rule #1 for avoiding rejection is to do your homework *before* you send your manuscript to an editor. *Read the magazine* if you're submitting to a journal. *Read the writers' guidelines* (these days both publisher and magazine writers' guidelines are easily accessible online) no matter where you're submitting. Submitting a manuscript to every editor whose magazine begins with "A" without looking at the magazines themselves is not only a waste of your time and money, but a waste of an editor's as well.

Rule #2 is that cleanliness is next to godliness. I'm continually amazed at the number of people who think that an editor's job is to clean up writers' mistakes. No. No. A thousand times: No. An editor's job is to make sure your already fabulous manuscript shines. If it hasn't been tidied up in the first place, an editor's not going to bother looking at it.

Rule #3 is to get out there and meet people in the business, either through a local writers' organization, at writers conferences, or in classes. And by "people in the business" I mean writers as well as editors and agents. I don't believe I am all that well connected, and yet, I can almost always point someone toward the right person if I'm asked the right question.

But the other part of Rule #3 is equally important: You are far more likely to get your foot in the proverbial door if someone knows you than if you're cold-calling. Even if your only meeting with an editor was a ten-minute pitch session in Gee-whiz-ville, if you send your (polished!) submission to her with a note that you were the guy wearing the red carnation at the Gee-Whiz Writers Conference, that editor may give your manuscript a closer look.

EVEN A GREAT MANUSCRIPT MAY BE REJECTED

I don't have to quote you the oft-repeated statistics: how many editors rejected Dickens, Hemingway, Fitzgerald, etc., before their works of genius were finally published to general acclaim. The thing is, editors are people and, hence, have subjective tastes. Besides *The Da Vinci Code*, which I already admitted I couldn't read (all right, I never got past the second page), the recent books I haven't liked are *The Time Traveler's Wife* (an admission that often provokes shouting) and *Extremely Loud and Incredibly Close*. I'm clearly in a minority, but I stand by my reckonings.

If I had been an editor and *The Da Vinci Code* had been sent to me, I would have suggested the author expand his characters beyond stereotypes and for God's sake lose the clichés. I can't say why I didn't care for *The Time Traveler's Wife*; perhaps it was just a victim of Wrong Book-Wrong Time Syndrome. In the case of *Extremely Loud and Incredibly Close*, though, I can say unequivocally that I have no patience with precocity, from which (in my opinion) the book suffers to the nth degree.

My point is that editors who reject your perfectly acceptable work will have likes and dislikes just like mine. They will also know fairly quickly if a manuscript is one they will want to read. How quickly? Most editors can tell by reading the first sentence. If they like that first sentence, they may reach the end of the first paragraph before changing their minds. If you've still got them by the end of the first paragraph, you've got a page to hook 'em for good.

HOOKED BUT SUNK

All this said, you will nonetheless get letters from editors that say, "Loved this. Please try us again," which leave you wondering why, if they loved it, they didn't buy it, for goodness sake.

The answer is that limited space I mentioned earlier. If it's between your untried story and one that Joyce Carol Oates offered gratis, guess which is going to win? This brings us back to Rule #3: It's Who You Know. So get thee to a writers conference. It will be more than worth the effort of getting out of your pajamas.

Try, Try Again

Rules be damned, the truth is it never gets any easier. I still receive rejections, although these days, they're from major book publishers to whom my agent has submitted my work, a fact that doesn't make them any easier to digest. In fact, I still feel like something one of the dogs dragged in each time it happens. (You don't want to see what the dogs really do drag in—or try to, till we stop them at the door.)

So, with this chapter's subject matter in mind, the story below is meant to be both encouraging and cautionary. Take from it what you will.

I GIVE UP

In the early 1990s, I sent out numerous short stories to magazine after magazine. I did my homework, reading the magazines first to determine each editor's particular sensibility. But, although I did have a few successes, by and large most of the stories came back with those form rejections (or worse, I realize in retrospect, "ink"—if they liked it, I always wondered, why didn't they buy it? My answer can now be found above, under the header "Hooked, But Sunk").

By 1995, I was sick of that punched-in-the-gut feeling I knew far too well, the one I got whenever I opened my mailbox to find an SASE inside, and I stopped sending out stories. I stopped writing them, too, focusing instead on novels and commissioned nonfiction books for the next five years. Then, in 2000, I saw a brief article in the *Albuquerque Journal* for the Jim Sagel Prize for the Novel. The award, the article said, would be given for an unpublished novel by a writer living in New Mexico, in memory of Jim Sagel, a New Mexico writer who'd died several years before. Not only was there a substantial cash prize, but, best of all (to me), there wasn't an entry fee.

With the deadline still several months away, I had time to consider which of the many novels stewing in my closet might be a candidate for such a prize. I finally settled on *Dissonance*, both because it was largely based in New Mexico and because I believed it was my strongest work to date.

I took the novel out of my closet, dusted it off, and sat down for a Marathon Read-Through. I found lots to like—and a great deal I felt needed improvement. After the Read-Through was over, I began typing in my edits. I trimmed, moved, and otherwise altered much of the music theory. I reconsidered and reconfigured the two main characters' trajectories. I did a lot of other miscellaneous nipping and tucking.

Finally, I printed out a new copy of the manuscript and sat down to read it once more. As I did, I realized that the novel fell into five sections.

And so the last thing I did before printing out the manuscript to send to the contest was add these divisions.

A year later, Kevin McIlvoy, the contest judge, called to say he'd selected *Dissonance* as the winner of the prize. I kid you not, my first thought was that it had won because I'd divided the manuscript into those five sections! Of course, I soon realized that it was everything I'd done that made it stand out from the other 150-plus entries—the Marathon Read-Through, the trimming, moving, nipping, and tucking.

But, in fact, my initial impulse wasn't all that far off the mark. Because when I divided the manuscript into those five sections (or rather, it did so itself), I was adding one last layer to the many the novel already had. Why? Because one of the two main characters is writing a symphony that stubbornly refuses to fall into four movements as symphonies usually do, but instead insists on being five. By dividing the novel into five (what I now call) movements, I was echoing one of the subtle threads of my fiction.

That's why I say that the last thing I do is make sure every thread is pulled tight. I don't want any loose threads hanging, showing, or marring my manuscript. Yes, it sounds like a lot of work, but the final product is worth it. Witness *Dissonance*: After it was published by the University of New Mexico Press in 2003, it went on to be chosen a book of the year by libraries across the country, was a selection of both NPR Performance Today's Summer Reading Series and Durango-La Plata County Reads!, and was a finalist for the PEN Southwest Book Award. None of that could have happened if I hadn't done the hard work of rereading, revisiting, revising, and rewriting my manuscript.

There are several lessons here, one about the importance of patience, another about the importance of revision and rewriting (which you already know very well is one of my favorite topics). But most important is what it says about a writer's self-confidence. Every time we think we can't set ourselves up for rejection yet again, we do. But if we've done the work, the hard job of editing and cutting and pasting and saying good-bye to the words we love best, ultimately, our self-confidence will be rewarded.

And yet, the next day (or the day after that), my confidence level plummeted back to zero. Yes, it happens to me, too. And I'd venture to say that it probably happens to Amy Tan and Sue Miller and Alice Munro, too (well, maybe not Alice Munro …). Writers—no, let's expand our equation to include all artists, because I know this happens to my daughter, who is a visual artist—have no middle ground when it comes to self-confidence. We're either cocky as all get-out or certain we're not worth scrubbing the pots with—and often, both at the same time.

I TRY AGAIN

So why do we do it? You've heard the usual answers: We write because we have to. We write because we have something to say. We write because if we didn't, we'd wonder if we really existed at all. But this self-confidence thing, and its lack, suggests there's more to it than even all those important reasons. So I'd say we write because we believe, and because we don't. It's not only part of being a writer; it's part of being human. We can't help but try, try again. It's an up-and-down life, but I wouldn't trade it for all the ink and paper in New York. Would you?

And so, my final words of wisdom to you are that it's my firm belief that if you do the hard work of revision and rewriting, you ultimately will see your name among those of published authors. I promise. Now, what are you waiting for? Start writing!

MINDING YOUR STORY
Rules for Avoiding Rejection

1. Do Your Homework.
2. Cleanliness Is Next to Godliness.
3. Get Out of Your Pajamas and Meet People in the Business.
4. Honor Thy Editors as Thou Would Wish to Be Honored.
5. Keep the Faith.

Appendixes

appendix a
"WILD HORSES"

{A} He told her where he was going and he told her when he'd be back. She smiled, and then asked him, Where are you going?

Althea, Althea, he thought as he eased his pickup up the rutted dirt track that was their drive. {B} He thought of how she'd point to the horses in the corral, the horses she'd bought and broke herself, and say, Those. What do you call them?

Horses, William answered her, each time, and Althea would nod, as if she knew he was wrong but would play along anyway.

Yes, she'd say. Those.

***

{C} Neighbors watched for her little pickup along the county road. Sometimes Althea would pull over, or not pull over, and stop. {D} Janet Kendall once found her sitting on her tailgate in the middle of the road just over a rise, had slammed on her brakes and skidded to a dusty halt just short of the rear bumper. What are you doing, Althea? Janet had asked, leaping from her car, heartsound still thrumping in her throat.

Why hello, Althea answered. What are *you* doing? I'm sorry I can't remember your name. I don't, sometimes.

Janet drove Althea and her pickup home and then stayed until William got home from work. She shouldn't be driving anymore, she told him as he drove her back to her car.

She's all right, William said.

She could get killed, said Janet.

William nodded thoughtfully. Yes, he said. I suppose she could. But she probably won't.

***

{E} Once a month he took her to the clinic in town. Oh! Pretty! Althea always said as they walked between the rows of wildflowers to the whooshing doors that led inside. In winter she cried, Look! Look at the lovely! The snow, she meant. Her delight in beauty had not changed at all; what William thought of as The Essential Althea was still very much present. He did not admit that The Essential Althea had loved to argue with him, or anyone, about absolutely anything.

{F} Her best friend, Betty Herbert, came over, and together they walked out to the corral. William stood at the window, jingling the change in his pockets. Betty handed Althea a saddle, which Althea held awkwardly, by a stirrup. Betty patted the saddle-blanket on Firefly's back. Althea tilted her head to one side and laughed. How amusing she found everyone, William thought, as if she knew the true way and everyone else were floundering.

***

{G} In the drought summer, fires burned on the mountains. At night, William and Althea sat on their deck and watched the orange glow two ridges over that was an out-of-control blaze near Durango. Pretty, Althea said, pointing. Sometimes she hummed, melodies William was certain he knew but could not name. Words would rise in his mind unbidden, words that were gone as soon as he realized they were there.

{H}The wild horses were dying. Several thousand of them roamed the BLM land that bordered their ranch, but the springs had dried up, and the graze was non-existent. Those near enough to their ranch stuck their scrawny necks through the fences and stole grass from their irrigated fields. At first William shooed them off, but Althea found them amusing and so he let them stay.

{I} Barnard from the BLM came by the Water District, where William worked as an engineer. Barnard was young and liberal, didn't believe there should be grazing permits or gas wells on the BLM land, but today he came to talk about the starving horses.

We're gonna hafta shoot 'em, he said. It's the only humane thing to do.

{J} William wondered if Althea was even now standing at the window, laughing to herself as the bony horses stretched their necks to reach the grass inside the fence.

{I}We need your permission, of course, Barnard went on. Your easement's our best way in.

William nodded, not agreeing, just listening. My wife loves those horses, he said. He didn't know if this was precisely true.

Barnard nodded back. Then she'll understand what we've got to do. I don't like it any better than you do, Nordstrom. But they shouldn't have to suffer.

Who's to say they're suffering? William asked. Barnard didn't answer, a small point in his favor.

***

{K}That night at the Alzheimer's Family Support Group, a woman talked about her mother in the nursing home. She can't remember the name for anything, the woman said, but her manners are impeccable. The group laughed in empathetic recognition.

I sometimes think my wife has found a better wisdom, William said into the silence that followed the laughter. He had not known he was going to speak—he seldom did, at these meetings—but as soon as he had he felt it was right.

The woman who had just finished her story nodded enthusiastically. There *is* this certain *acceptance*, she said. It's nearly—*beatific*. I mean, my mother never approved of a damned thing I did till she lost her memory. The group laughed again.

My wife is a very strong-willed person, said William. Very strong-willed, and *smart*. He hesitated, trying to think of words for what he suddenly knew he believed. The only thing that's changed is that instead of fighting, she's agreeing. It's like living with a saint.

If Althea could hear me, he thought, she'd laugh her ass off. The old Althea, that is.

***

{L} The old Althea had been made of spit and barbed wire, as she liked to say. She was one of a breed of women not so rare in the West as they liked to think, a college-educated rancher. Her B.A. was in English (*Very practical*, she'd say with one eyebrow raised), and she sometimes taught at the high school, in lean years. She could recite Wordsworth from memory, and liked to read obscure modern poets while she cooked supper. Sometimes she'd read a passage aloud to William. He could never think of a thing to say, when she finished.

But her first love was horses; she was a woman who had never outgrown her girlhood crush. Horses didn't come before William, or their daughter Barbara, but they were close. Althea had a talent for picking them, breaking them, training them, and for letting them go. It was the last that most impressed William, the way she could load her closest companion of two years onto a stranger's trailer and walk back to the house to start supper, never once looking over her shoulder.

***

{M} Barnard had called the house while William was at the meeting. Althea answered but the machine had already picked up, and, home again, William listened to their conversation, feeling as if he were eavesdropping.

{N} Hello, Althea said, a statement.

Mrs. Nordstrom? This is Hank Barnard? BLM? We met at the Christmas party at the bank?

How nice, Althea said. I don't remember you.

Barnard described himself. Not very well, William thought.

And what's your name? Althea asked.

Barnard told her.

I don't know you, do I? William wondered if Barnard was going to go through the whole thing again. He was the type of person Althea had never liked—All dogma, no substance, was the way she put it—and leading him around and around this particular ring was an exercise she would have relished.

But Barnard must have figured something out. Tell William I called, he said. About the horses.

Why yes! exclaimed Althea. They're called horses! The machine cut off Barnard's response.

***

{M} Barbara had called, too, and William called her back first. She was crying when she answered. She didn't know who I was, Dad.

It's not you, honey. It's her.

But I'm her daughter, Barbara wailed. William could not understand how their daughter, a therapist in San Diego, could be so relentlessly insecure.

She's actually very happy, William said. She loves watching the wild horses.

My God, Barbara said. They've come all the way in? She said it as if they were bears or cougars.

They're starving, said William. The BLM wants to come in and shoot them.

Well, they should, Barbara said. It's awful to let them starve that way.

Who are we to decide that? William asked.

Dad, Barbara said in her therapist voice. Don't you weird out, too, okay?

I'm fine, William said.

***

{O} Harold Cheskie found Althea wandering in his pasture, walking between two cows, a hand resting easily on each broad back. His wife Thelma left a message on the machine to that effect, not wanting to disturb William at work, she said, and Althea would be at their place so why didn't William just come up for dinner, she was making a rack of lamb and there'd be plenty for him and Althea both.

{P} Harold was as silent as Thelma was loquacious, but over coffee he turned to William and said, You got to do something with her.

Should I take her out to the barn and shoot her? William said with a laugh.

Althea, humming, was inspecting the veins on the back of her hand, tracing them carefully with her index finger, and Thelma reached across and lifted her untouched coffee out of the way, then turned to William.

She can't be left alone, William. We all watch out for her, you know we do, but we can't watch all the time, we've got our own lives to live. What if she'd of gotten in with the bulls instead of the cows, or what if she got near them wild horses you're just letting roam by your fence-line?

They won't hurt her, William said.

Well, maybe they won't, but Harold's bulls would, and I wouldn't want that weight on my shoulders. Thelma paused. You need to do something, William. My girl Theresa's a nurse at the hospital, she might know someone could come in, if you're not ready for the other yet. I could call her. I *will* call her. I'll see if she knows someone. That settled, she offered more coffee.

***

{Q} They hadn't known about the wild horses when they first bought the ranch; Althea discovered them a few years later when she was breaking an Appaloosa stallion down in the canyon on the BLM land.

There's hundreds of them, she told William that evening. Gorgeous things, blacks and bays, dapples and greys. William thought he heard a melody behind the words, a nursery rhyme, long forgotten. But what he asked was if she were going to break them. He pictured his lovely young wife astride a white stallion, bareback, holding lightly to the horse's mane with one hand.

Althea had given him the You Are So Incredibly Dense look. I wouldn't think of breaking them, William. They're wild. They're free.

***

{R} Barnard came by with his supervisor, a man from Denver in a denim shirt with the store creases still showing. Creases explained how they were going to shoot the horses no matter what, but that they'd sure appreciate William's cooperation.

Sure, William said. Sure. Do what you gotta do.

***

{S} That night the smoke from the fires was so thick they couldn't see the lights of town. Far off on the BLM, starving horses nickered weakly back and forth, while above them invisible planes ferried slurry to the burn, now only one ridge away, then hurried back to Junction for another load. The slurry drops burst pink in the southeast sky, as if an alien spaceship were landing.

Pretty, Althea said, pointing. Humming.

{T} The next morning William unlocked the gate and let three BLM Jeeps through. They didn't bother with the horses by the fence, but went on down into the canyon, their route marked by a receding plume of dust.

{U} They heard the first shots about noon. The horses by the fence exchanged glances and then went back to grazing. Althea tilted her head like a collie and resumed watching, or not watching, television. William stood by the window, though he couldn't see anything. He thought about the bodies, which he knew they'd leave in the canyon for the coyotes. Mostly bones anyway, Barnard had said.

Another volley of shots echoed up. Althea looked at him and smiled. You should sit, she said, patting the couch next to her. The—she gestured at her ear—it's not so bad then.

William sat. Then he lay his head in Althea's lap and cried and cried, while Althea patted his hair, and hummed a tune he'd never heard before and now would hear forever after.

appendix b

MANUSCRIPT PAGE
IN PROGRESS

ask: if he thought their father would still be alive tomorrow. Another day won't matter, will it?

she rephrased.

I guess not, Lester said.

So, is he awake much? Janet asked. What does he say? Does he ask for me?

Mostly, he sleeps, answered Lester. When he's awake, he just wants to hold Mom's hand.

Sometimes he says he feels lousy. He told Eleanor he was happy she was there. He's called her

Janet more than once. You can tell she doesn't like that one bit.

He asks for me? Janet said. What does he say?

Another nickel, said the operator.

I'll call tomorrow, Lester squeezed in before he was cut off.

Janet sighed, then stood to depress the switch-hook and dial Arnold at the store. Marv

answered. Hey good lookin', he said, just as he always did. Whatcha got cookin'?

Janet sighed. Marv might be married to her best friend Shirley but right now she just

couldn't begin to have this ridiculous conversation, which annoyed her in the best of times, yet

again. Is Arnold there? she asked.

In the back, Marv said. Everything okay? Your Pop all right?

Marv? Janet pleaded. Arnold?

Sure thing, sure thing, Marv said, dropping the phone onto the counter with a clunk. She

heard his footsteps receding and a moment later his and Arnold's, coming back.

Honey? Arnold said. Everything okay?

I think we should go, Janet said. To Cleveland.

That's fine, Arnold said. We can leave in the morning.

I can't leave in the morning, you know that. Tomorrow afternoon, maybe?

Lisa Lenard-Cook   Beautiful Dreamer   Page 21

appendix c

SCRIBBLE SHEET

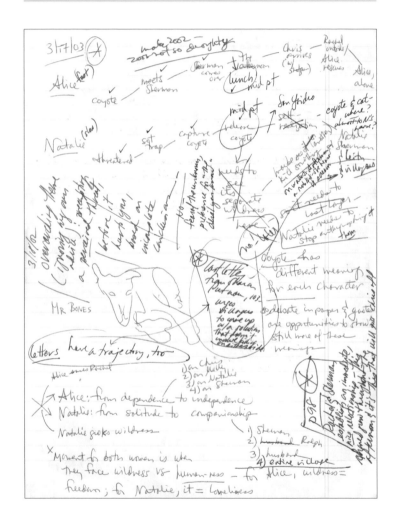

appendix d
BIBLIOGRAPHY

Books on Writing

Bernays, Ann and Pamela Painter. *What If?* New York:
HarperPerennial, 1990.

Bluestone, George. *Novels Into Film.* Berkeley: University
of California, 1968.

Cameron, Julia. *The Artist's Way.* New York: Tarcher, 1992.

Campbell, Joseph. *The Power of Myth.* New York: Anchor, 1991.

Edwards, Betty. *Drawing on the Right Side of the Brain.* New York:
Tarcher, 1989.

Forster, E.M. *Aspects of the Novel.* New York: Harcourt, 1927.

Freed, Lynn. *Reading, Writing, and Leaving Home.* New York:
Harcourt, 2005.

Goldberg, Natalie. *Writing Down the Bones.* Boston: Shambhala, 1986.

Harper Collins Music Dictionary, The, 2nd ed. New York:
HarperPerennial, 1991.

King, Stephen. *On Writing.* New York: Scribner, 2000.

Lamott, Anne. *Bird by Bird.* New York: Pantheon, 1994.

Lessing, Doris. *A Small Personal Voice.* New York: Vintage, 1975.

Lukeman, Noah. *The Plot Thickens.* New York: St. Martin's, 2002.

Macauley, Robie and George Lanning. *Technique in Fiction.*
New York: St. Martin's, 1990.

Neubauer, Jay. *Conversations with Writers.* New York:
HarperPerennial, 1994.

Oates, Joyce Carol. *(Woman) Writer.* New York: E.P. Dutton, 1998.

Welty, Eudora. *One Writer's Beginnings.* New York: Warner, 1984.

White, E. B. *The Elements of Style,* 3rd ed. New York: McMillan, 1979.

Fiction

Auster, Paul. *The Book of Illusions.* New York: Picador, 2003.

Chabon, Michael. *Wonder Boys.* New York: Picador, 1995.

Chandler, Raymond. *The Big Sleep.* New York:
The World Publishing Co., 1939.

Didion, Joan. "Last Words," *The New Yorker,* Nov 9, 1998.

Dreiser, Theodore. *Sister Carrie.* New York: Modern Library, 1927.

Eliot, George. *Adam Bede.* New York: Belford, Clarke, and Co, 1886.

Fitzgerald, F. Scott. *The Great Gatsby.* New York: Amereon, 1925.

Freeman, Judith. *Red Water.* New York: Anchor, 2003.

Giles, Molly. *Creek Walk and Other Stories.* New York: Scribner, 1998.

Haddon, Mark. *The Curious Incident of the Dog in the Night-Time.* New
York: Vintage, 2004.

Hemingway, Ernest. *A Farewell to Arms.* New York:
Charles Scribner's Sons, 1929.

James, Henry. *The Golden Bowl.* New York:
Charles Scribner's Sons, 1914.

Lee, Harper. *To Kill a Mockingbird.* New York: Lippincott, 1960.

Lenard-Cook, Lisa. *Coyote Morning.* Albuquerque:
University of New Mexico Press, 2004.

___. *Dissonance.* Albuquerque: University of New Mexico Press, 2003.

___. *Keep It Simple Guide to Dreams,* DK: 2003.

___. "Men on White Horses." *Southwest Review* 91:1, January 2006.

___. "Wild Horses."

Lively, Penelope. *Moon Tiger*. London: Penguin Books Ltd., 1998.

McInerney, Jay. *Bright Lights, Big City*. New York: Vintage, 1984.

Melville, Herman. *Moby-Dick*. New York, Modern Library, 1992.

Miller, Sue. *While I Was Gone*. New York, Ballantine, 2000.

Minot, Susan. *Evening*. New York: Vintage, 1999.

Munro, Alice. "Runaway." *Runaway*. New York: Vintage, 2005.

Nabokov, Vladmir. *Lolita*. New York: G.P. Putnam's, 1955.

Porter, Katherine Anne. "The Jilting of Granny Weatherall,"
    The Old Order. New York: HBJ, 1969.

Rodgers and Hammerstein. *Oklahoma!*, 1945.

Salinger, J.D. *The Catcher in the Rye*. New York: Little Brown, 1951.

Shakespeare, William. *Hamlet*. In *Shakespeare, The Complete Works*.
    New York: Random House, 1952.

Shields, Carol. *Unless*. New York: Fourth Estate, 2002.

Simpson, Mona. *Anywhere But Here*. New York: Vintage, 1988.

Styron, William. *Sophie's Choice*. New York: Random House, 1979.

INDEX